W9-BFP-222

PIONEERS IN MATHEMATICS

MATHEMATICS FRONTIERS

1950 to the Present

MICHAEL J. BRADLEY, PH.D.

CHELSEA HOUSE
PUBLISHERS
An imprint of Infobase Publishing

Mathematics Frontiers: 1950 to the Present

Chelsea House
An imprint of Infobase Publishing
132 West 31st Street
New York NY 10001

Library of Congress Cataloging-in-Publication Data

Bradley, Michael J. (Michael John), 1956–
   Mathematics frontiers : 1950 to [the] present / Michael J. Bradley.
     p. cm.—(Pioneers in mathematics)
   Includes bibliographical references and index.
   ISBN 0-8160-5427-4 (acid-free paper)
   1. Mathematicians—Biography. 2. Mathematics—History—20th century.
I. Title.
   QA28.B7357 2006
   510.92'2—dc22   2005036154

Text design by Mary Susan Ryan-Flynn
Cover design by Dorothy Preston
Illustrations by Jeremy Eagle

Printed in the United States of America

MP FOF 10 9 8 7 6 5 4 3 2 1

This book is printed on acid-free paper.

CONTENTS

CHAPTER 10

Sarah Flannery (1982–): New Algorithm for

PREFACE

Mathematics is a human endeavor. Behind its numbers, equations, formulas, and theorems are the stories of the people who expanded the frontiers of humanity's mathematical knowledge. Some were child prodigies while others developed their aptitudes for mathematics later in life. They were rich and poor, male and female, well educated and self-taught. They worked as professors, clerks, farmers, engineers, astronomers, nurses, and philosophers. The diversity of their backgrounds testifies that mathematical talent is independent of nationality, ethnicity, religion, class, gender, or disability.

Pioneers in Mathematics is a five-volume set that profiles the lives of 50 individuals, each of whom played a role in the development and the advancement of mathematics. The overall profiles do not represent the 50 most notable mathematicians; rather, they are a collection of individuals whose life stories and significant contributions to mathematics will interest and inform middle school and high school students. Collectively, they represent the diverse talents of the millions of people, both anonymous and well known, who developed new techniques, discovered innovative ideas, and extended known mathematical theories while facing challenges and overcoming obstacles.

Each book in the set presents the lives and accomplishments of 10 mathematicians who lived during an historical period. *The Birth of Mathematics* profiles individuals from ancient Greece, India, Arabia, and medieval Italy who lived from 700 B.C.E. to 1300 C.E. *The Age of Genius* features mathematicians from Iran, France, England, Germany, Switzerland, and America who lived between the 14th and 18th centuries. *The Foundations of Mathematics* presents 19th-century mathematicians from various European countries. *Modern Mathematics* and *Mathematics Frontiers* profile a variety of international mathematicians who worked in the early 20th and the late 20th century, respectively.

The 50 chapters of Pioneers in Mathematics tell pieces of the story of humankind's attempt to understand the world in terms of numbers, patterns, and equations. Some of the individuals profiled contributed innovative ideas that gave birth to new branches of mathematics. Others solved problems that had puzzled mathematicians for centuries. Some wrote books that influenced the teaching of mathematics for hundreds of years. Still others were among the first of their race, gender, or nationality to achieve recognition for their mathematical accomplishments. Each one was an innovator who broke new ground and enabled their successors to progress even further.

From the introduction of the base-10 number system to the development of logarithms, calculus, and computers, most significant ideas in mathematics developed gradually, with countless individuals making important contributions. Many mathematical ideas developed independently in different civilizations separated by geography and time. Within the same civilization, the name of the scholar who developed a particular innovation often became lost as his idea was incorporated into the writings of a later mathematician. For these reasons, it is not always possible to identify accurately any one individual as the first person to have discovered a particular theorem or to have introduced a certain idea. But then mathematics was not created by one person or for one person; it is a human endeavor.

ACKNOWLEDGMENTS

An author does not write in isolation. I owe a debt of gratitude to many people who helped in a myriad of ways during the creation of this work.

To Jim Tanton, who introduced me to this fascinating project.

To Jodie Rhodes, my agent, who put me in touch with Facts On File and handled the contractual paperwork.

To Frank K. Darmstadt, my editor, who kept me on track throughout the course of this project.

To Mary Lee Goguen, who helped research the material for the chapter on Sarah Flannery.

To Constance Reid, who generously provided a picture of Julia Robinson and suggested changes that improved this and other chapters.

To Fan Chung, who provided pictures of herself and of Paul Erdös.

To John Tabak, Kit Moser, and Tucker McElroy, who shared helpful suggestions for locating sources of photographs and illustrations.

To Kevin St. John, Graeme Griffith, Craig Looney, and Russ Pinizzotto, who provided valuable comments and additional information for several chapters.

To Steve Scherwatzky, who helped me become a better writer by critiquing early drafts of many chapters.

To Melissa Cullen-DuPont, who provided valuable assistance with the artwork.

To my wife, Arleen, who helped find photographs and patiently provided love and support throughout this three-year project.

To Christina Condon, Patricia Paquette, and the other members of the McQuade Library staff at Merrimack College who helped me obtain access to essential books and articles.

To the many relatives, colleagues, students, and friends who inquired and really cared about my progress on this project.

To Joyce Sullivan, Donna Katzman, and their students at Sacred Heart School in Lawrence, Massachusetts, who created poster presentations for a math fair based on some of these chapters.

To the faculty and administration of Merrimack College who created the Faculty Sabbatical Program and the Faculty Development Grant Program, both of which provided me with time to read and write.

INTRODUCTION

Mathematics Frontiers, the fifth volume of the book set Pioneers in Mathematics, profiles the lives of 10 mathematicians of the second half of the 20th century. Each has left his or her own mark, but collectively they constitute a cross section of the international mathematics community during an era when that community became more diverse and when the United States emerged as a leading center for mathematical research. This period of years also witnessed the resolutions of many long-standing open problems, significant developments in both pure and applied mathematics, and the introduction of new mathematical ideas that made possible major technological advances.

The mathematicians profiled in this volume exemplify a growing diversity within the mathematical community. The advancement of mathematical knowledge today draws on the talents of individuals from all nationalities, races, ethnicities, and genders. This particular group of women and men from the United States, Great Britain, Hong Kong, Taiwan, Belgium, and Ireland are representative of the broader international community of scholars.

During the latter half of the 20th century, the United States rose to prominence within the international mathematical community. The Institute for Advanced Study in Princeton, New Jersey, emerged as a leading research center, attracting many of the world's top mathematicians for extended periods of collaboration. The establishment of strong research groups at many U.S. universities and at industrial sites such as Bell Laboratories in New Jersey drew prominent scholars from around the world and fostered the development of talented young people. Although only three of the

10 mathematicians profiled in this book were born in the United States, eight of them spent or have spent the majority of their careers at American institutions.

Several of these mathematicians solved problems that had resisted solution for many years. Julia Robinson's work of more than 20 years with Diophantine equations produced research results that were essential in solving Hilbert's 10th problem, a question that mathematicians had been investigating since the beginning of the 20th century. Shing-Tung Yau solved the Calabi conjecture about geometrical properties of surfaces and many other open problems in differential geometry. In one of the most celebrated mathematical achievements of the century, Andrew Wiles proved Fermat's last theorem, a problem that had remained unsolved for more than 300 years.

Mathematicians in the 20th century made significant discoveries in both pure and applied mathematics. John H. Conway helped complete the classification of all finite groups, invented the Game of Life, and performed extensive mathematical analysis of other games of strategy. J. Ernest Wilkins, Jr., developed techniques for radiation shielding to guard against the effects of the gamma rays produced by nuclear reactions. Stephen Hawking established the mathematical basis for black holes and other advanced theories in mathematical physics. John Nash won the Nobel Prize in economics for his introduction of Nash equilibrium for cooperative and noncooperative games.

Advances in mathematics made possible many of the technological developments of the electronic age. Fan Chung developed an encoding and decoding algorithm for cellular telephone calls and analyzed aspects of the mathematical structure of the network of computers that forms the Internet. Ingrid Daubechies's development of Daubechies wavelets led to new image processing techniques for fingerprint analysis, computer animation, and medical imaging. Sarah Flannery developed a new cryptographical method for securely and efficiently transmitting coded messages.

The 10 individuals profiled in this volume represent the thousands of scholars who have made modest and momentous mathematical discoveries that have advanced the world's knowledge. The stories of their achievements provide a glimpse into the lives and the minds of some of the pioneers in mathematics.

Julia Robinson

(1919–1985)

Julia Robinson formulated the Robinson hypothesis and proved key theorems about exponential Diophantine equations that were essential to the solution of Hilbert's 10th problem. *(Courtesy of Constance Reid)*

Discoveries in Number Theory and Mathematical Logic

Working for most of her professional career without a full-time faculty appointment, Julia Robinson made significant discoveries in mathematical logic and number theory. The theorems she proved about decision problems in rings and fields contributed new results to mathematical logic. In number theory her formulation of the Robinson hypothesis and her proofs of key theorems about exponential Diophantine equations were essential to the solution of Hilbert's 10th problem. She became the first woman mathematician to be elected to the National Academy of Science, serve as president of the American Mathematical Society, and receive the MacArthur Foundation Prize for contributions to mathematics.

Student of Mathematics

Julia Hall Bowman was born on December 8, 1919, in St. Louis, Missouri, to Ralph Bowers Bowman, the owner of a machine tool and equipment business, and Helen Hall Bowman, a business college graduate. When her mother died in 1922, Julia and her older sister, Constance, went to live with their grandmother in a small desert community near Phoenix, Arizona. A year later her father sold his business and moved to Arizona with his second wife, Edenia Kridelbaugh, a former schoolteacher. In 1925 the family moved to Point Loma, California, where Julia attended the local elementary school until the age of nine, when she contracted scarlet fever, rheumatic fever, and chorea. After spending a year in bed at the home of a practical nurse and another year recuperating at her family's new home in San Diego, she worked with a tutor three mornings a week and within 12 months had successfully mastered the curriculum for grades five through eight.

In addition to pistol and rifle shooting, horseback riding, and art, Bowman developed a deep interest in mathematics that evolved during her years in high school and college. When she graduated from San Diego High School in 1936, she won the school's awards for mathematics, biology, and physics as well as general excellence in science. At the age of 16 she entered San Diego State College, intending to pursue her certification as a teacher of mathematics. Upon reading Eric Temple Bell's book *Men of Mathematics* for a course on the history of mathematics, however, she became fascinated by the idea of mathematical research and developed an interest in number theory. After her junior year she transferred to the University of California at Berkeley to pursue a career as a research mathematician.

At Berkeley Bowman became a member of a large, supportive community of mathematics students and faculty members. She graduated with a bachelor's degree in mathematics in 1940 and enrolled in Berkeley's graduate program, where she was elected to the honorary mathematics fraternity. During her first year of graduate studies she worked for the Russian statistician Jerzy Neyman as a laboratory assistant in the Berkeley Statistical Laboratory, and in 1941 she completed her master's degree in mathematics. She passed the civil service examination to become a junior statistician but declined the offer of a position as a night clerk in Washington, D.C., deciding instead to continue her graduate studies in mathematics. During her second year of graduate school she obtained a teaching assistantship to teach introductory statistics. In December 1941 she married Raphael Robinson, who had been her professor for a number theory course during her first year at Berkeley. Because university regulations prohibited a husband and a wife from teaching for the same department, she worked on military projects as a research assistant in the Berkeley Statistical Laboratory during World War II, while continuing to audit graduate mathematics classes. Her work at the "stat lab" led to her first publication, a 1948 paper titled "A Note on Exact Sequential Analysis," which appeared in the *University of California Publications in Mathematics*. In this paper she presented a new proof of a recently published result on the statistical analysis of sequences of numbers.

Decision Problems in Arithmetic

While spending the academic year 1946–47 at Princeton University in New Jersey, where her husband was a visiting professor, Robinson became interested in problems in the area of mathematical logic, the branch of mathematics dealing with formal argumentation and consistent reasoning about abstract structures. When she returned to Berkeley in 1947, she started a doctoral program under the direction of Polish logician Alfred Tarski. In June 1948 she earned her Ph.D. for a dissertation titled "Definability and Decision Problems in Arithmetic," which was published the following year in the *Journal of Symbolic Logic*. Her research extended the work of Tarski and Moravian-born American logician Kurt Gödel. In his 1931 undecidability theorem for the arithmetic of natural numbers, Gödel had proven that there could not be a single algorithm capable of deciding the truth of every statement involving addition, multiplication, elementary logic, and variables representing positive integers. In 1939 Tarski had shown that the arithmetic of real numbers is decidable by proving that there was an algorithm to determine the truth of such statements about real numbers. Robinson's dissertation proved that the arithmetic of rational numbers—numbers that can be written as fractions of two integers—was undecidable by showing that every equation involving rational numbers could be transformed into an equation involving integers by an algorithm with finitely many steps. Although mathematicians have continued to work on this problem, no one has improved on Robinson's result that the arithmetic of rational numbers is adequate for the formulation of all problems of elementary number theory and that the rational number field is algorithmically unsolvable.

In subsequent years Robinson continued this line of research, publishing three additional papers on decision problems in mathematical logic. Her 1959 paper "The Undecidability of Algebraic Rings and Fields," published in the *Proceedings of the American Mathematical Society*, extended the results of her dissertation to decision problems for more general mathematical structures known as rings and fields. In her 1962 paper "On Decision Problems for Algebraic Rings," appearing in *Studies in Mathematical Analysis and Related Topics: Essays in Honor of George Pólya*, she showed that rings of integers of various fields of algebraic numbers are undecidable. At the 1963 International Symposium at Berkeley, she presented further results in a paper titled "Definability and Decision Problems in Rings and Fields," published in 1965 in the monograph *The Theory of Models*. Her work enabled other mathematicians to show that the decision problem for arbitrary number fields was unsolvable.

Game Theory and Politics

From 1949 to 1950 Robinson worked as a junior mathematician at RAND Corporation in Santa Monica, California, where she investigated strategies for finite two-person zero-sum games in which two competing participants make choices that result in a payoff for one player and a penalty of equal magnitude for the other. She developed an iterative solution for the value of the "fictitious play" problem in which each player utilizes an optimal strategy in response to all the opponent's moves so far. In her paper "An Iterative Method of Solving a Game," which was published in 1951 in *Annals of*

Mathematics, she proved that as the number of plays increases, the payoffs for the two players will converge to the value of the game. This paper, her only work in this branch of mathematics, remains a fundamental result in game theory more than 50 years later.

Throughout the 1950s Robinson continued her involvement in a number of endeavors outside her primary area of research in mathematics. In 1951–52 she worked as an applied mathematician at Stanford University under a grant from the Office of Naval Research performing research on hydrodynamics, the study of the properties of fluids in motion. When the administrators of California's state universities required all employees to sign an anticommunism loyalty oath, Robinson worked to support the faculty members who had lost their jobs for refusing to comply. She became deeply involved in Democratic Party politics, actively working for Illinois governor Adlai Stevenson's unsuccessful 1952 and 1956 presidential campaigns. In 1958 she served as a county campaign manager for Alan Cranston who was elected as state controller.

Hilbert's 10th Problem

While pursuing her diverse interests, Robinson continued to engage in mathematical research in the area of number theory, the branch of mathematics concerned with the properties of the positive integers. The primary focus of her research for most of her mathematical career was Diophantine analysis, the area of number theory that deals with methods for finding integer solutions of polynomial equations with integer coefficients. In 1900 German mathematician David Hilbert had proposed a set of 23 problems that he viewed as central to the progress of mathematics during the 20th century. The 10th problem on his list challenged mathematicians to find an algorithm to determine if a given Diophantine equation had any integer solutions. From 1948, when she first started working on Hilbert's 10th problem, to 1976, when she published her last paper on the subject, she made a number of significant discoveries that were indispensable to the resolution of this problem.

Robinson's initial contributions to the solution of Hilbert's 10th problem involved recursive functions, functions in which the value at each positive integer is defined in terms of its values at smaller positive integers. In 1950 at the International Congress of Mathematicians at Harvard University in Cambridge, Massachusetts, she presented a brief talk entitled "General Recursive Functions" that was later published in the *Proceedings of the American Mathematical Society*. In this paper she proved that all general recursive functions of one variable can be obtained from two special primitive recursive functions by two operations known as composition and inversion. She discovered additional properties of recursive functions and recursively defined sets in several later papers.

In her 1952 paper "Existential Definability in Arithmetic," published in the *Transactions of the American Mathematical Society*, Robinson proved several important results about existential definability and exponential functions. A set of positive integers is existentially definable if a parameter in a solvable Diophantine equation generates all the values in the set. Exponentiation is the higher-order operation, more sophisticated than addition and multiplication, in which the power or exponent in an algebraic expression is a variable rather than a fixed number. In this paper Robinson proved that the binomial coefficients, the factorials, and the prime numbers are existentially definable in terms of exponentiation. She also proved that the exponential relation $x = y^z$ is existentially definable in terms of any function that demonstrates roughly exponential growth. By broadening the scope of the investigation beyond polynomial Diophantine equations to exponential Diophantine equations, this paper made a major contribution to the solution of Hilbert's 10th problem.

From 1959 to 1961 Robinson collaborated with U.S. researchers Martin Davis and Hilary Putnam to produce a result that brought them within one step of the complete solution of Hilbert's 10th problem. In 1959 Davis and Putnam sent Robinson an early draft of a paper they were writing about exponentiation and recursive sets. Robinson helped simplify the proof and strengthen the theorem by removing one of the restrictive conditions. Their collaborative efforts resulted in the paper "The Decision Problem for Exponential Diophantine Equations" that appeared in 1961 in the *Annals of Mathematics*. In this paper they proved that every recursively enumerable set is existentially definable in terms of exponentiation. As a consequence of this result, they showed that there is no algorithm for deciding if an exponential Diophantine equation has integer solutions.

In this paper Robinson proposed a conjecture known as the Robinson hypothesis in which she theorized that there exists a Diophantine equation that grows faster than a polynomial but not as fast as an exponential function. If true, exponentiation would be existentially definable, exponential Diophantine equations would be equivalent to polynomial Diophantine equations, and there-fore the answer to Hilbert's 10th problem would be negative—it would be impossible to create an algorithm to determine if a given Diophantine equation had integer solutions. At the 1960 International Congress on Logic, Methodology, and Philosophy of Science, she presented their joint work in a paper titled "The Undecidability of Exponential Diophantine Equations."

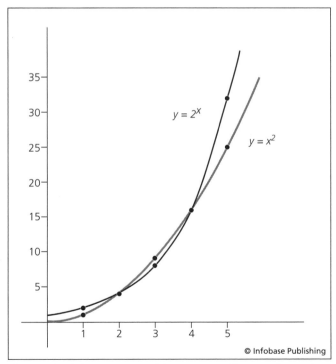

© Infobase Publishing

The graph of the exponential function $y = 2^x$ grows faster than the graph of the polynomial function $y = x^2$. The Robinson hypothesis that formed the essential step in the solution of Hilbert's 10th problem conjectured that there exists a Diophantine equation that grows faster than a polynomial but not as fast as an exponential function.

Robinson underwent heart surgery in 1961 to remove scar tissue related to her childhood bout with rheumatic fever. After the surgery her health improved so that she could enjoy bicycling, hiking, and canoeing and could teach one graduate mathematics course per year as a part-time lecturer at Berkeley. She became a frequent participant at number theory conferences, presenting papers about her continuing work on Diophantine equations. In her 1968 paper "Recursive Functions of One Variable," which appeared in the *Proceedings of the American Mathematical Society*, she showed that all general recursive functions can be obtained from two functions known as the zero function and the successor function by using the operation of composition and the technique of general recursion. The same journal published her related research in a 1968 paper titled "Finite Generation of Recursively Enumerable Sets" and her 1969 papers "Finitely Generated Classes of Sets of Natural Numbers" and "Unsolvable Diophantine Problems." She also wrote summary articles that surveyed the current status of research on Hilbert's 10th problem. Two of these were her 1969 article "Diophantine Decision Problems," which appeared in *Studies in Number Theory*, and her presentation at the 1969 Summer Institute on Number Theory at Stony Brook, New York, titled "Hilbert's Tenth Problem."

In January 1970, 22-year-old Russian mathematician Yuri Matijasevich provided the final step in the solution of Hilbert's 10th problem by discovering a Diophantine equation that satisfied the Robinson hypothesis. He showed that the relation $n = F_{2m}$, where F_{2m} is the $2m$th element of the sequence of Fibonacci numbers $1,1,2,3,5,8,13,21, \ldots$, can be expressed as a polynomial Diophantine equation involving n, $2m$, and other integer-valued variables. Matijasevich's construction of this example provided the necessary existential definition of a Diophantine relation that grows faster than a polynomial but not as fast as an exponential function, as Robinson had conjectured. Having completed the solution of Hilbert's 10th problem, Robinson, Matijasevich, Davis, and Putnam joined the "Honors Class" of mathematicians who earned international recognition by solving Hilbert's problems.

After the negative resolution of this famous question, Robinson started to investigate other properties of Diophantine equations. At the Fourth International Congress on Logic, Methodology, and Philosophy of Science held in 1971 in Bucharest, Romania, she presented a paper titled "Solving Diophantine Equations" in which she classified Diophantine equations for which known methods provided integer solutions. In her 1973 paper "Axioms for Number Theoretic Functions," which appeared in *Selected Questions of Algebra and Logic*, she gave a finite set of axioms for number-theoretic functions from which the Peano axioms can be derived.

Initiating a research collaboration with Matijasevich, Robinson succeeded in developing methods to reduce the number of variables needed in a Diophantine equation. In their 1974 paper "Two Universal Three-Quantifier Representations of Enumerable Sets," published in the Russian journal *Theory of Algorithms and Mathematical Logic*, they proved that the relation of exponential growth could be defined using only three variables. The following year their joint paper "Reduction of an Arbitrary Diophantine Equation to One in 13 Unknowns" published in *Acta Arithmetica* showed how any Diophantine equation could be rewritten as an equivalent equation using at most 13 variables. Matijasevich later succeeded in reducing the necessary number of variables to nine. He insisted that Robinson be listed as a coauthor of this discovery in recognition of her contributions to the methods used, but Robinson refused to accept any credit for the improved result. As a consequence, the discovery was not published until 1982 when Canadian mathematician James Jones included it in his paper "Universal Diophantine Equation" in the *Journal of Symbolic Logic*.

Robinson, Matijasevich, and Davis collaborated on a 1974 paper titled "Hilbert's Tenth Problem. Diophantine Equations: Positive Aspects of a Negative Solution." Robinson presented this paper in May 1974 at the Symposium on Hilbert's Problems held at Northern Illinois University in De Kalb. The paper presented a nontechnical introduction to many results obtained by mathematical logicians in connection with Hilbert's 10th problem. Published in 1976 in the conference proceedings, titled *Mathematical Developments Arising from Hilbert's Problems*, this article was her final published paper.

Honors and Service to the Profession

From 1976 to 1985 Robinson spent most of her time working in service to her professional colleagues and accepting honors that her role in the solution of Hilbert's 10th problem had merited. In 1976 she was elected to the National Academy of Sciences (NAS). That same year the University of California at Berkeley, where she had been teaching as a part-time lecturer, appointed her to their permanent faculty as a full professor with a reduced teaching load. In 1978 she was elected vice president of the American Mathematical Society (AMS) and was inducted into the American Association for the Advancement of Science.

Two professional mathematical societies honored Robinson by asking her to deliver major lectures at national conferences. In 1980 the AMS invited her to present the prestigious Colloquium Lectures at their 84th summer meeting at the University of Michigan in Ann Arbor. Her four lectures, collectively titled "Between Logic and Arithmetic," addressed the spectrum of her interests in mathematical logic and number theory: Gödel's work and the concept of computability, Hilbert's 10th problem and exponential Diophantine equations, decision problems for various rings and fields, and nonstandard models of arithmetic. The Association for Women in Mathematics (AWM) named her their Emmy Noether Lecturer for the Joint Mathematics Meetings in Cincinnati, Ohio, in January 1982. At that conference thousands of mathematicians from the Society of Industrial and Applied Mathematics, the Mathematical Association of America, the AMS, and the AWM gathered to hear her lecture "Functional Equations in Arithmetic."

Over the next few years the AMS and other organizations continued to recognize Robinson's achievements. In 1982 her mathematical colleagues elected her to become the president of the AMS. During her term of office as president-elect in 1982–83 and president in 1983–84, she worked to support programs that provided greater opportunities for women and underrepresented minorities in mathematics and the sciences. In 1983 she was awarded the John D. and Catherine T. MacArthur Foundation Prize for contributions to mathematics, an award that provided her an annual research stipend of $60,000 for five years. In 1985 the American Academy of Arts and Sciences elected her to membership. That same year the Council of Scientific Society Presidents elected her as their chair, but she declined due to her failing health.

On July 30, 1985, after a yearlong battle with leukemia, Robinson died at the age of 65. To honor her memory San Diego High School instituted the Julia Robinson Prize in Mathematics, an annual award presented to the outstanding mathematics student in the graduating class. Her husband established the Julia B. Robinson Fellowship Fund to provide fellowships for graduate students in mathematics at Berkeley. These memorial awards encourage and enable talented young people to pursue their interests in mathematics.

Conclusion

Before she died, Julia Robinson asked that she be remembered not as the first woman to receive particular honors or to be elected to certain offices but rather for the problems she solved and the theorems she proved. Although she was the first woman mathematician to be elected to the NAS, to serve as president of the AMS, and to win the MacArthur Foundation Prize, she earned her reputation as a research mathematician by the significance of her discoveries in mathematical logic and number theory. The results she obtained in her doctoral dissertation and subsequent research papers about decision problems in rings and fields contributed new discoveries to the understanding of decision problems in mathematical logic. Her conjecture of the Robinson hypothesis and her proofs of key theorems about exponential Diophantine equations proved to be essential steps in the resolution of Hilbert's 10th problem.

FURTHER READING

Hall, Loretta. "Julia Bowman Robinson, 1919–1985, American Logician and Number Theorist." In *Notable Mathematicians: From Ancient Times to the Present*, edited by Robyn V. Young, 421–423. Detroit, Mich.: Gale, 1998. Brief but informative profile of Robinson and her work.

Henderson, Harry. "Julia Bowman Robinson (1919–1985)." In *Modern Mathematicians*, 103–111. New York: Facts On File, 1996. Biographical profile with a discussion of her most important discoveries.

Henkin, Leon, et al. "Julia Bowman Robinson, 1919–1985." *Notices of the American Mathematical Society* 32 (1985): 738–742. Personal reflections by 13 colleagues on their relationships with Robinson.

O'Connor, J. J., and E. F. Robertson. "Julia Hall Bowman Robinson." MacTutor History of Mathematics Archive, University of Saint Andrews. Available online. URL: http://www-groups.dcs.st-andrews.ac.uk/~history/Mathematicians/Robinson_Julia.html. Accessed January 27, 2003. Biography provided by the University of Saint Andrews, Scotland.

Reid, Constance. "The Autobiography of Julia Robinson." *College Mathematics Journal* 17 (1986): 2–21. "Autobiography" written by her sister constituting the primary source of biographical information.

———. "Being Julia Robinson's Sister." *Notices of the American Mathematical Society* 43 (1996): 1,486–1,492. Article in a mathematics journal providing additional insight into selected events in her life.

———. *Julia: A Life in Mathematics.* Washington, D.C.: American Mathematical Society, 1996. Book-length work presenting a reprint of her "autobiography," many additional photographs, and three articles about her work written by her colleagues Lisl Gaal, Martin Davis, and Yuri Matijasevich.

———. "Julia Robinson." In *More Mathematical People*, edited by Donald J. Albers, Gerald L. Alexanderson, and Constance Reid, 262–280. Boston: Harcourt, Brace, Jovanovich, 1990. Reprint of "autobiography" from *College Mathematics Journal.*

Reid, Constance, with Raphael M. Robinson. "Julia Bowman Robinson (1919–1985)." In *Women of Mathematics: A Biobibliographic Sourcebook*, edited by Louise S. Grinstein and Paul J. Campbell, 182–189. New York: Greenwood Press, 1987. Biographical profile with an evaluation of her mathematics and an extensive list of references, written by her sister and her husband.

Riddle, Larry. "Julia Bowman Robinson." Agnes Scott College. Available online. URL: http://www.agnesscott.edu/lriddle/women/robinson.htm. Accessed January 27, 2003. Article about Robinson's life and work.

Smorynski, C. "Julia Robinson, In Memoriam." *Mathematical Intelligencer* 8, no. 2 (1986): 77–79. Article in a mathematics journal providing a description of her dissertation and her work on Hilbert's 10th problem, with some biographical information.

J. Ernest Wilkins, Jr.

2

(1923–   )

J. Ernest Wilkins, Jr., conducted mathematical research on the zeros of random polynomials and helped develop radiation shields to guard against the harmful effects of gamma rays. *(Courtesy of Dan Dry, University of Chicago Alumni Magazine)*

Mathematician, Scientist, and Engineer

In his productive 60-year career, J. Ernest Wilkins, Jr., earned national recognition for his contributions to mathematics, science, and engineering. He was among the first African Americans to earn a doctoral degree in mathematics, have an appointment at the Institute for Advanced Study, and be elected to the National Academy of Engineering. His mathematical research contributed to differential equations, advanced calculus, geometry, function theory, and the study of polynomials. He designed optical instruments for space telescopes and heat fins to cool engines. His most significant achievements—his discoveries about gamma-ray penetration and the distribution of neutron energies—were important for designing nuclear power plants and radiation shields.

Early Achievements

Jesse Ernest Wilkins, Jr., was born in Chicago on November 23, 1923, to J. Ernest Wilkins, Sr., and Lucille Robinson Wilkins. A successful attorney, Ernest's father served as president of the Cook County Bar Association, the professional society of African-American lawyers in the cities and towns near Chicago. In the 1950s he achieved national prominence when President Dwight D. Eisenhower appointed him to the Civil Rights Commission and to the position of assistant secretary of labor. After graduating from college, Ernest's mother earned a master's degree and pursued a career as a teacher in the Chicago schools. Ernest's younger brothers, John and Julian, both earned law degrees and joined their father's legal practice.

As a young child Wilkins demonstrated advanced mental abilities, reciting the alphabet when he was only 13 months old and learning how to add, subtract, multiply, and divide by the age of five. In elementary school his score of 163 on an IQ test classified him as a genius. A competitive person, he mastered the card game of blackjack when he was seven and a few years later won his community's Ping-Pong championship.

In school Wilkins established a record of academic distinction. Excelling in all his subjects, he finished high school four years early and, at the age of 13, became the youngest student ever to enroll at the University of Chicago. There his professors selected him for membership in Phi Beta Kappa, the oldest and most respected national honor society for college students. In the William Lowell Putnam Mathematical Competition, a national problem-solving contest sponsored by the Mathematical Association of America, he finished among the top-10 competitors in the country. In 1940, at the age of 16, he graduated from college with a bachelor's degree in mathematics.

The University of Chicago invited Wilkins to continue his education and pursue a doctoral degree in mathematics. To earn this degree, a student must take additional courses and conduct research to prove a new theorem or rule in mathematics. After completing a year of advanced courses, Wilkins earned a master's degree in mathematics in 1941. In the next year and a half, he completed specialized high-level mathematics courses and worked with his research adviser Magnus Hestenes to develop a technique that could be used to solve some problems from advanced calculus. He presented the results of his research in his dissertation "Multiple Integral Problems in Parametric Form in the Calculus of Variations." In December 1942, a few weeks after his 19th birthday, Wilkins became the eighth African American to earn a doctoral degree in mathematics.

Mathematics Professor

The School of Mathematics at the Institute for Advanced Study (IAS) in Princeton, New Jersey, offered Wilkins a postdoctoral fellowship to be one of eight mathematicians conducting research for the year 1942–43 at the country's most prominent institution for mathematics. He embraced this opportunity, becoming only the second African-American mathematician to receive a visiting appointment at the IAS. Devoting his full-time efforts to his research, Wilkins discovered new results in advanced geometry and wrote papers describing his findings. In 1943 the *Duke Mathematical Journal* published his first two research papers: "The First Canonical Pencil" and "A Special Class of Surfaces in Projective Differential Geometry."

After his postgraduate year at the IAS, Wilkins had difficulty obtaining a position as a college mathematics professor. The only institutions willing to hire an African-American faculty member were the few colleges and universities in the South that are often referred to as the "historically black colleges and universities" (HBCUs). These schools had been established primarily to educate African-American men and women because most institutions of higher learning refused to accept them as students. One of these institutions, Tuskegee Institute in Alabama, hired Wilkins as a professor in its mathematics department for the year 1943–44. Although he was younger than some of his students, his knowledge of mathematics and his concern for their education earned their respect. In addition to his teaching, he continued his research developing new theories and techniques to solve problems in differential equations, advanced calculus, advanced geometry, statistics, and the spread of diseases. Six mathematics journals published seven of his research papers on these topics in the next two years. These included "On the Growth of Solutions of Linear Differential Equations," published in 1944 in the *Bulletin of the American Mathematical Society*; his dissertation, published in 1944 in the *Annals of Mathematics*; "A Note on Skewness and Kurtosis," published in 1945 in the *Annals of Mathematical Statistics*; and "The Differential Difference Equation for Epidemics," published in 1945 in the *Bulletin of Mathematical Biophysics*.

Scientist and Engineer

Although Wilkins's early achievements indicated that he would become a successful mathematical researcher and college professor, he left the academic world and spent the next 26 years working in industry and on government-sponsored research projects. From 1944 to 1946 he worked as a physicist at the University of Chicago's Metallurgical Laboratory (Met Lab), where researchers were developing techniques to change uranium into radioactive plutonium, a process that generated incredible heat. Wilkins helped develop methods for cooling the equipment that produced the radioactive substances. His work at Met Lab was part of the Manhattan Project, the U.S. government program to develop a powerful atomic bomb. This massive scientific research project brought together the talents of thousands of the best mathematicians, scientists, and engineers in the world, including 21 scientists who would receive the Nobel Prize, the highest recognition for achievement in science.

In 1946 Wilkins joined the American Optical Company in Buffalo, New York. For four years he worked as a mathematician helping design space-probing telescopes. The designs of the sophisticated lenses required a knowledge of the curves known as conic sections as well as other advanced ideas from geometry and physics. He continued to conduct mathematical research, discovering new results in function theory, geometry, differential equations, and advanced calculus. Ten of his research papers on these subjects were published in mathematics journals. These included "The Isoperimetric Problem of Bolza with Finite Side Conditions," published in 1947 in the *Bulletin of the American Mathematical Society*; "A Note on the General Summability of Functions," published in 1948 in the *Annals of Mathematics*; "Neumann Series of Bessel Functions," published in 1948 in the *Transactions of the American Mathematical Society*; and "The General Term of the Generalized Schlömilch Series," published in 1950 in the *American Journal of Mathematics*. In 1947 he married Gloria Stewart; in the next few years the couple had a daughter, Sharon, and a son, J. Ernest Wilkins III.

Wilkins experienced another incident of racial discrimination in 1947 when he planned to attend a professional meeting of the American Mathematical Society (AMS) at the University of Georgia, with hundreds of other mathematicians and math professors. When the organizers of the conference learned that he was a black man, they informed him that he would not be allowed to stay in the same hotels or eat in the same restaurants as the white mathematicians. Instead, they had arranged for him to stay with and have his meals with a black family who lived nearby. Angered that he was being treated as a second-class citizen, Wilkins canceled his travel plans, and for many years he refused to attend mathematics conferences in the South.

Gamma Rays

For the next 20 years Wilkins worked to develop peaceful uses of nuclear reactions. In 1950 he joined a group of six other scientists at Nuclear Development Corporation of America (NDA) in White Plains, New York. In his roles as senior mathematician, manager of physics and mathematics, director of research and development, and a major stockholder in the corporation, he helped make important decisions about the company's future as it grew into an organization of more than 300 scientists during the next 10 years.

Wilkins and his NDA colleague Herbert Goldstein studied the process of fission in which the nucleus of an atom gives off high-energy and low-energy rays. Through a series of experiments, they discovered that the high-energy gamma rays penetrate through certain materials and not through others. Their work, announced in the 1953 paper "Systematic Calculations of Gamma-Ray Penetration" in the journal *Physical Review*, was important for designing nuclear reactors that generate electric power. These discoveries were also crucial in the development of radiation shields that protect astronauts and their equipment from gamma rays and other high-energy particles that are produced by nuclear reactions that take place in the Sun.

Working with Nobel Prize–winning scientist Eugene Wigner, Wilkins determined how to predict the quantity of high-energy and low-energy rays that would be absorbed by different materials during a nuclear reaction. Their work, called the Wigner-Wilkins approach to estimating the distribution of neutron energies, was an important step in the development of nuclear fuel that could be used to produce electricity or to power a submarine or a spacecraft. Wilkins presented this work on neutron absorption to other scientists at the 1956 International Conference on Peaceful Uses of Atomic Energy.

In addition to his groundbreaking research and his other responsibilities at NDA, Wilkins continued his education. For two-and-a-half years he attended evening classes at New York University, earning a bachelor's degree in mechanical engineering in 1956. He graduated with honors, was elected to the two honorary engineering societies Pi Tau Sigma and Tau Beta Pi, and received the award for the most promising graduating engineer. Three years later, at the age of 37, he earned his master's degree in mechanical engineering from the same university.

From 1960 to 1970 Wilkins continued his research on nuclear energy at the Atomic Division of General Dynamics Corporation in San Diego, California, where he progressed from assistant chairman of theoretical physics and assistant director of defense science and engineering to director of computational research. One of his projects during these years involved cooling nuclear-powered engines. Nuclear reactions generate incredible heat that can be directed away from the engine by attaching metal fins known as heat sinks. He used his knowledge of mathematics to determine what shape the fins should be to draw the most heat from the engine. The

1961 paper "Minimum-Mass Thin Fins with Specified Minimum Thickness," published in the *Journal of the Society for Industrial and Applied Mathematics*, was one of many papers and technical reports that detailed the results of his research.

Professor Again

In 1970 Wilkins returned to the academic world, accepting a position as distinguished professor of applied mathematical physics at Howard University in Washington, D.C. He taught his students how to use the theories and techniques of mathematics and physics to solve applied problems in optics, nuclear power, and other branches of science and engineering. His new research interests, which spanned gambling strategies, linear systems, roots of polynomials, Hilbert spaces, and multiple integrals, generated eight more articles in mathematics journals. Among these were "The Bold Strategy in Presence of House Limit," published in 1972 in the

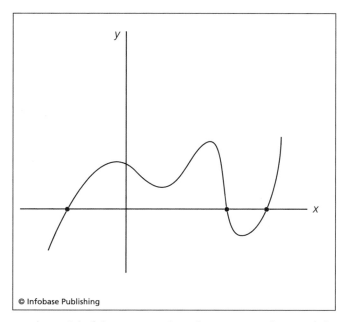

© Infobase Publishing

A polynomial of degree n can have between 0 and n roots where its graph intersects the horizontal axis. Wilkins analyzed the average number of roots that resulted when the coefficients of the polynomial were randomly selected.

Proceedings of the American Mathematical Society; "An Upper Bound for the Expected Number of Real Zeros of a Random Polynomial," published in 1973 in the *Journal of Mathematical Analysis Applied;* and "A Variational Problem in Hilbert Spaces," published in 1975 in *Applied Mathematics of Optimization.*

In addition to his research and teaching, Wilkins worked with James Donaldson, the chairman of Howard's mathematics department, to address the reality that very few African Americans were earning graduate degrees in mathematics. Together they organized a doctoral program, and in 1976 Howard University became the first HBCU to offer a Ph.D. in mathematics. Beyond the boundaries of the university's campus, Wilkins continued to be active in professional communities. He served as president of the American Nuclear Society in 1974–75 and was a council member of the AMS from 1975 to 1977.

Wilkins left Howard University and spent the years 1977 to 1984 at EG&G Idaho, a large engineering firm in Idaho Falls. In his position as vice president and deputy general manager for science and engineering, he coordinated projects involving nuclear science and optics. His research papers "Minimum Critical Mass Nuclear Reactors, Part I and Part II," published in 1982 in *Nuclear Science and Engineering,* discussed critical aspects involved in the design and operation of nuclear reactors. In "Apodization for Maximum Critical Irradiance of Resolution, II," published in 1984 in the *Journal of the Optical Society of America A: Optics and Image Science,* he presented his work on the design and manufacture of optical equipment. He spent the year 1984–85 as a visiting scientist at the Argonne National Laboratory, the new name of Met Lab where he had worked on the Manhattan Project 30 years earlier. By this time the focus of work at the facility had become research on the peaceful uses of nuclear energy for the U.S. Department of Energy.

Temporary Retirement

Wilkins retired in 1985 but five years later joined the faculty at Clark Atlanta University in Georgia as a distinguished professor of applied mathematics and mathematical physics. In his 13 years at this institution, another of America's HBCUs, he taught his students to use mathematics to solve problems from the areas of science and engineering to which he had devoted his career. At mathematics conferences he talked to students from other universities about careers in math and science. In 1992 he made a videotape for the AMS, *Optimization of Extended Surfaces for Heat Transfer*, in which he explained how he used mathematics to design the cooling fins for nuclear-powered engines. Continuing his own mathematical research on the roots of polynomials with random coefficients, he wrote six more papers, including "Mean Number of Real Zeros of a Random Trigonometric Polynomial," published in 1991 in the *Proceedings of the American Mathematical Society*, and "The Expected Value of the Number of Real Zeros of a Random Sum of Legendre Polynomials," published in 1997 in the same journal. In 2003, at the age of 79, he retired again and moved back to his hometown of Chicago.

Conclusion

Throughout his distinguished career, Wilkins has received honors and awards for his achievements in three different fields—science, engineering, and mathematics. In 1956, at the age of 32, he was elected a fellow of the American Association for the Advancement of Science in recognition of the significance of his research on gamma rays and radiation shields. He was elected a fellow of the American Nuclear Society in 1964 in honor of his work in the field of nuclear engineering. In 1976 the National Academy of Engineering acknowledged the importance of his work on the design and development of nuclear reactors for generating electrical power by making him their second African-American member. The United States Army awarded him the 1980 Outstanding Civilian Service Medal. The National Association of Mathematicians (NAM) gave him its lifetime achievement award in 1994 and established an annual lecture series named in his honor. Every year a different mathematician is selected to present his or her work in this, the most important lecture at NAM's annual undergraduate mathematics conference.

During his 60-year career as a mathematician, a scientist, and an engineer working for universities, the government, and private companies, J. Ernest Wilkins, Jr., produced more than 100 technical reports and research papers in science, engineering, and mathematics journals. His discoveries on gamma rays and radiation shielding have had significant impacts on the aerospace, nuclear medicine, and nuclear power industries. Mathematical researchers continue to develop his ideas from advanced calculus, advanced geometry, and function theory.

FURTHER READING

Houston, Johnny L. "J. Ernest Wilkins, Jr." Strengthening Underrepresented Minority Mathematics Achievement (SUMMA) Program of the Mathematical Association of America. Available online. URL: http://www.maa.org/summa/archive/WilkinsJ. htm. Reprint of Houston's biography of Wilkins originally published in the Fall 1994 newsletter of the National Association of Mathematicians. One of 50 online biographies of minority mathematicians.

Moite, Sally M. "J. Ernest Wilkins, Jr., 1923– , African-American Mathematical Physicist." In *Notable Mathematicians: From Ancient Times to the Present*, edited by Robyn V. Young, 517–518. Detroit, Mich.: Gale, 1998. Brief but informative profile of Wilkins and his work.

O'Connor, J. J., and E. F. Robertson. "Jesse Ernest Wilkins Jr." MacTutor History of Mathematics Archive, University of Saint Andrews. Available online. URL: http://www-groups.dcs.st-andrews.ac.uk/~history/Mathematicians/Wilkins_Ernest.html. Accessed July 30, 2003. Biography provided by the University of Saint Andrews, Scotland.

Tubbs, Vincent. "Adjustment of a Genius: Ex-Prodigy J. Ernest Wilkins Jr., Now Top Nuclear Scientist, Has Normal Family Life." *Ebony*, February 1958, pp. 60–67. Magazine article with biographical content; for general audiences.

Williams, Scott W. "J. Ernest Wilkins, Jr." Mathematicians of the African Diaspora, Mathematics Department of the State University of New York at Buffalo. Available online. URL: http://www.math.buffalo.edu/mad/PEEPS/wilkns_jearnest. html. Accessed August 3, 2005. One of 500 online biographies of African-American mathematicians.

John Nash

3

(1928–)

John Nash's introduction of the concept of Nash equilibrium for cooperative and noncooperative games won him a Nobel Prize in economics. *(Reuters/CORBIS)*

Nobel Prize—Winning Game Theorist

John Nash won the Nobel Prize in economics for his work in game theory. His introduction of the concept of Nash equilibrium for cooperative and noncooperative games significantly impacted the development of game theory and revealed widespread applications to economics, biology, and political science. His innovative research on the imbedding of manifolds and the analysis of fluid flows established his reputation as a creative and promising young mathematician. He endured a 30-year struggle with mental illness to return to his research in the 1990s.

Education and Early Years

John Forbes Nash, Jr., was born on June 13, 1928, in Bluefield, West Virginia, to John Forbes Nash, Sr., an electrical engineer with Appalachian Power Company, and Margaret Virginia Martin, an English and Latin teacher. Both parents were well educated: his father earned a bachelor's degree from the Agricultural and Mechanical College of Texas (now Texas A&M University), and his mother studied languages at Martha Washington College and West Virginia University. Nash and his younger sister, Martha, attended the local public schools and received additional tutoring at home from their parents.

As a boy Nash developed interests beyond the standard school curriculum. A shy child with underdeveloped interpersonal skills, he preferred to read books and perform experiments with electricity, chemicals, and explosives rather than play sports or attend social events. At school he discovered nonstandard methods for solving mathematical problems that were superior to the techniques his teachers taught. Reading Eric Temple Bell's book *Men of Mathematics*, he became interested in the lives of research mathematicians and worked out the proofs of some classic results in number theory. During his senior year of high school, he took additional mathematics courses at Bluefield College. With his father, Nash, at the age of 17, authored the paper "Sag and Tension Calculations for Cable and Wire Spans Using Catenary Formulas," which was published in the journal *Electrical Engineering* in 1945. The article described an improved method for calculating the proper tensions for electric cables and wires, a project that had entailed weeks of field measurements followed by mathematical analysis.

In 1945 Nash won one of 10 George Westinghouse Scholarships in a national competition and entered Carnegie Institute of Technology (now Carnegie-Mellon University) in Pittsburgh, Pennsylvania. Originally enrolled in a degree program in chemical engineering, he changed his major to mathematics after taking courses in tensor calculus and relativity. He competed twice in the William

Lowell Putnam Mathematical Competition, a national problem-solving contest for college students sponsored by the Mathematical Association of America, but he considered it a failure that he did not rank among the top five students in the country either year. As an undergraduate, he independently reproved the Brouwer fixed-point theorem, the principle from algebraic topology that any continuous function on the surface of an *n*-dimensional sphere must map at least one point back into itself. While taking a course in international economics, he sketched out original ideas on bargaining strategies that formed the basis of a paper he published in 1950.

After earning both a bachelor's degree and a master's degree in mathematics in 1948, Nash applied to graduate schools to pursue his doctoral degree in mathematics. In a one-sentence letter of recommendation, his mathematics professor Richard J. Duffin wrote that Nash was a genius. He turned down offers from the graduate programs at Harvard University, the University of Chicago, and the University of Michigan to accept a prestigious John S. Kennedy Fellowship from Princeton University in New Jersey.

In September 1948 Nash entered Princeton, where he pursued broad interests in several branches of pure mathematics, including topology, algebraic geometry, game theory, and mathematical logic. He seldom attended lectures or read the recommended textbooks, preferring instead to rediscover mathematical properties independently from fundamental principles, a habit that helped him develop original methods of inquiry and unique perspectives on problems. In the common room of the dormitory he frequently played games of logic and strategy, including chess, Go, and Kriegspiel. He invented a topological game similar to Hex that the other graduate students called "Nash."

Revolutionizing Game Theory

During a three-year period, from 1948 to 1951, Nash wrote a doctoral dissertation and four research papers that revolutionized game theory, the branch of mathematics dealing with the study of competition and cooperation. In the 1920s Hungarian mathematician John von Neumann had analyzed two-person, zero-sum games in which two competing participants made choices that resulted in a payoff for one player and a penalty of equal magnitude for the other. In von Neumann's later papers and the 1944 book *Theory of Games and Economic Behavior* that he coauthored with Princeton economist Oskar Morgenstern, von Neumann had applied the formal mathematical theory of games to the field of economics. Nash broadened the scope of game theory to include situations with more than two participants and the analysis of general strategies for games in which players can either cooperate or compete with one another. He introduced concepts, tools, and techniques that became fundamental components in the full development of game theory and that enabled game theory to be broadly applied to evolutionary biology, economic theory, and political strategies.

Nash's first published work on game theory was a two-page paper titled "Equilibrium Points in n-Person Games" that appeared in 1950 in the *Proceedings of the National Academy of Sciences*. Completed during his first 14 months at Princeton and submitted to the academy in November 1949, this brief work introduced the definition of an n-person, finite, noncooperative game, a game with more than two competitors in which each player selects one of finitely many strategies without consulting the other players in order to obtain an outcome that is personally advantageous. Using the Brouwer fixed-point theorem, Nash concisely proved that in any such game, there exists at least one strategic equilibrium, or a collection of strategies, one for each player, having the property that if all players follow these strategies, no individual player can improve his or her outcome by switching to a different strategy. The idea of strategic equilibrium, now known as Nash equilibrium, has become the most widely used solution concept in game theory. Nash equilibriums produced the same results as von Neumann's technique for two-person, zero-sum games and addressed a more general class of games in which stable sets, a necessary feature of von Neumann's analysis, did not always exist.

The work presented in his first game theory paper formed the central idea of Nash's doctoral dissertation "Non-Cooperative Games," which he wrote under the direction of his research adviser, Albert W. Tucker. In this unpublished 27-page paper that he defended in May 1950, he more fully explained the general theory of noncooperative n-person games and provided a more detailed proof that every such game must have at least one Nash equilibrium point. As a concrete example of an equilibrium point, Nash and fellow graduate student Lloyd Shapley used Nash's ideas to analyze a three-handed game of poker. When Tucker recommended that Nash not include the application in his dissertation, he and Shapley instead published their joint work in the paper "A Simple Three-Person Poker Game" that appeared later in 1950 in the *Annals of Mathematical Studies.*

In his dissertation Nash introduced two interpretations of equilibrium points for rational and mass action games. He defined a rational game as a game that is played only once and in which the participants reason logically from knowledge of the full structure of the game. In a mass action game the game is repeatedly played by participants who do not necessarily act rationally and who may not know the full structure of the game but who accumulate information on the relative advantages of the available strategies. The mass action concept did not appear in any of his published papers but was independently discovered in the 1970s by biologists studying evolutionary strategies in which the process of natural selection achieves equilibrium by driving organisms toward the maximization of fitness. In economics the theory of mass action provided a mathematical basis for the principle of "survival of the fittest," which asserts that under market conditions, only companies that maximize their profits will survive in the long run.

In late 1950 Nash's paper titled "The Bargaining Problem" was published in *Econometrica*, a journal of mathematical economics. In this work he introduced a solution concept for two-person, cooperative games with fixed threats known as the Nash bargaining solution. For games involving two participants who agree in advance to pursue a mutually advantageous course of action and to accept specified penalties for deviating from the agreed-upon behavior, a Nash bargaining solution provided a resolution of the problem that was satisfactory to both players. Nash had developed some of the basic ideas for this paper while taking an economics course during his undergraduate years at Carnegie Institute of Technology. He produced a more sophisticated treatment of the problem at Princeton during the spring semester of 1949. By introducing four axioms, or basic principles, that any solution would have to satisfy, he proved the existence of a unique solution that maximized the collection of outcomes for the players. The editors of the journal that published the paper were unable to persuade him to replace an example involving two children bargaining over a bat, a ball, a toy, and a knife with a more sophisticated situation.

The paper also introduced the concept of a Nash bargaining game, a simple two-person game in which each player demanded a portion of an available resource. If the sum of the two players' demands did not exceed the total value of the resource, both players received what they had requested; otherwise, both players received nothing. Nash showed that any pair of numbers that added up to the total value of the resource constituted one of the infinitely many equilibrium points. He also explained that the alternative resources available to the two players and the consequences of obtaining no benefit from the game introduced many rational alternatives in addition to the obvious "50-50" split of the resource. The paper became a classic in economic theory and impacted international negotiation strategies.

In 1951 the *Annals of Mathematics* published Nash's paper "Non-Cooperative Games." One section of this paper extended portions of his dissertation by elaborating additional ideas about Nash equilibriums and providing a new proof of their existence based on Shizuo Kakutani's fixed-point theorem. The major contribution of this article was its introduction of the "Nash Program," a call by the author to reformulate cooperative games into the larger framework of noncooperative games. Nash reasoned that a cooperative game together with its preplay negotiation or bargaining process among the players constituted a larger noncooperative game. This realization unified the mathematical analysis of both types of games.

The last of Nash's five seminal works on game theory was his 1953 paper "Two-Person Cooperative Games," which appeared in *Econometrica*. He had originally intended to present the ideas from this paper in a section of his dissertation, but his adviser, Tucker, had recommended that he remove the topic from an early draft of the work. In this paper he more fully developed his ideas on Nash bargaining solutions for games with fixed threats that he had discussed in his "Bargaining" paper and presented Nash bargaining solutions for games with variable threats. Nash showed that with rational players, a variable threats game—a game in which a player can select one of a choice of penalties when the opponent deviates

	Player 2	
	A	B
a	1, 2	−1, −4
b	−4, −1,	2, 1

Player 1

In a 1951 paper Nash gave this example of a two-person noncooperative game having two equilibrium points. The payoff matrix indicates that if player 1 uses strategy *a* and player 2 employs strategy *A*, player 1 will earn a reward of 1 unit and player 2 will receive a reward of 2 units. Nash showed that although both (*a, A*) and (*b, B*) were equilibrium points, in practice both players usually avoid the penalty of −4 resulting in a tendency toward state (*a, A*).

from the agreed-upon strategy—reduces to a fixed threat game, with each player employing an optimal threat strategy. In contrast to traditional economic theory, Nash's paper showed that the rational division of an economic surplus leads to a unique outcome rather than being dependent on the players' negotiation skills.

Nash's dissertation and four published papers on game theory impacted developments in mathematics, economics, politics, and biology. His ideas encouraged game theorists to develop the mathematical theories of cooperative and noncooperative games independently and under the unified umbrella of noncooperative models. Economists used Nash equilibrium as a precise mathematical approach to analyzing human behavior in diverse competitive situations. His ideas on cooperative and noncooperative games reshaped modern economic theory. Governmental and military leaders used his ideas to analyze strategies for diplomatic negotiations and international military conflicts. In contrast to the typical pattern of the acceptance and the use of mathematical ideas, the concept of Nash equilibrium flowed gradually from the social sciences to the natural sciences, where 20 years later biologists started to use his work to understand the logic of animal and plant evolution and interaction.

Research on Manifolds and Fluid Flows

Within the international mathematical community Nash acquired a reputation as a talented researcher with original ideas. Although his work on game theory had brought him some recognition, he earned his reputation as a research mathematician primarily for the results he obtained in the 1950s on embeddings of manifolds and the analysis of continuous fluid flows. After receiving his doctoral degree from Princeton in 1950, he remained at the university for a year as an instructor. In 1951 he accepted a two-year appointment as a C. L. E. Moore Instructor in the Department of Mathematics at the Massachusetts Institute of Technology (MIT) in Cambridge, where he became an assistant professor in 1953. Although his unorthodox methods of teaching and examining made him unpopular with the students, his broad-ranging research on real algebraic varieties, Riemannian geometry, parabolic and elliptic equations, and partial differential equations earned him the respect of his colleagues.

As a graduate student at Princeton in 1949, Nash had made substantial progress on the solution of a problem from algebraic geometry, the branch of mathematics concerned with the study of the roots of polynomial equations. He had considered the theorem to be an alternative dissertation topic had his work on game theory not been accepted by the mathematics department. In this alternate research, Nash was trying to prove that any member of a broad category of geometrical surfaces known as manifolds was closely related to an algebraic variety, or a surface defined by a polynomial equation in a higher-dimensional space. After presenting a preliminary report titled "Algebraic Approximations of Manifolds" at the International Congress of Mathematicians held at Harvard University in September 1950, Nash spent an additional year completing the work. The final paper, titled "Real Algebraic Manifolds," which appeared in the November 1952 issue of the *Annals of Mathematics*, represented a significant contribution to algebraic geometry. His result surprised other mathematicians who had considered manifolds to be more complicated objects than algebraic varieties. His work enabled mathematicians to study manifolds and functions related to them by analyzing the zeros of polynomials.

During the next two years Nash further developed his result, leading to two additional papers on isometric imbeddings, maps from a manifold to a higher-dimensional space that preserve the distances between corresponding pairs of points in both spaces. In a seminar at Princeton in the spring of 1953, he presented a method for imbedding a Riemannian manifold into a three-dimensional Euclidean space. His paper "C^1 Isometric Imbeddings" describing this method appeared in the November 1954 issue of *Annals of Mathematics*. The imbedding preserved the measurement of distances between points but introduced irregularities known as singular points where the new surface had undesirable properties. By the time the paper was published, Nash had resolved the difficulties and had submitted a more detailed paper titled "The Imbedding Problem for Riemannian Manifolds," which appeared in the January 1956 issue of *Annals of Mathematics*. His two-part technique involved an iterative procedure for finding roots of a polynomial equation followed by a smoothing technique to remove the singularities. Nash's imbedding theorem introduced new techniques for solving the set of partial differential equations that arose in the process, an ingenious innovation that Russian geometer Mikhail Gromov described as a "lightning strike." Princeton mathematician John H. Conway classified Nash's imbedding theorem as one of the most important pieces of mathematical analysis in the 20th century. When German mathematician Jürgen Moser modified Nash's technique and applied it to celestial mechanics in 1966, the method became known as the Nash-Moser theorem.

In addition to his work on manifolds, Nash investigated hydrodynamics, the study of the properties of fluids in motion. In 1954 the *Bulletin of the American Mathematical Society* published his paper "Results on Continuation and Uniqueness of Fluid Flow" in which he used partial differential equations—equations involving the derivatives of functions of several variables—to analyze the irregular motion of fluid dynamics. He obtained a Sloan Fellowship that allowed him to spend the academic year 1956–57 at the Institute for Advanced Study (IAS) in Princeton and to visit other research mathematicians at New York University's Courant Institute of Mathematical Sciences. During this year he completed research that resulted in the conference presentation "Parabolic Equations," published in 1957 in the *Proceedings of the National Academy of Sciences*, and the more detailed paper "Continuity of Solutions of Parabolic and Elliptic Equations," which appeared in 1958 in the *American Journal of Mathematics*. In these papers he developed existence, uniqueness, and continuity theorems for parabolic and elliptic equations. He introduced another innovative approach by transforming nonlinear differential equations into simpler linear equations that he then solved by nonlinear means. Although his breakthrough attracted much attention, including the offer of an appointment at the Courant Institute, he was disappointed when he learned that the Italian mathematician Ennio De Giorgi had recently obtained the same result by different means in the case of elliptic functions.

From 1950 to 1954 Nash also worked as a consultant to the RAND Corporation, a research and development agency in Santa Monica, California, funded by the United States Air Force. He produced a collection of technical reports and memorandums analyzing applications of game theory to military and diplomatic strategies. In August 1950 he submitted a report titled "Rational Nonlinear Utility" and the memorandum "Two-Person Cooperative Games" that led to his 1953 publication on games involving threats. His 1952 memo "Some Games and Machines for Playing Them" discussed the computerization of game-playing algorithms. With RAND colleague Robert M. Thrall he coauthored the 1952 memo "Some War Games" that analyzed potential military applications of game theory. With Gerhard Kalisch and Evar D. Nering, two RAND researchers from the University of Michigan, and John W. Milnor, a colleague from Princeton, he cowrote a 1954 report that was published in the book *Decision Processes* under the title "Some Experimental *n*-Person Games." This joint work reported on the results of a bargaining experiment involving hired subjects that led to foundational work in the field of experimental economics. His 1954 RAND memos "Higher Dimensional Core Arrays for Machine Memories," "Continuous Iteration Method for Solution of Differential Games," and "Parallel Control" focused on computer applications of game theory. Nash lost his security clearance and was dismissed from RAND in 1954 after police arrested him on charges of illicit behavior.

Struggles with Paranoid Schizophrenia

From the late 1950s through the late 1980s, Nash's life and promising career deteriorated into a lengthy struggle with mental illness interrupted by occasional periods of mathematical insight. He married his former student Alicia Esther Larde in February 1957, and MIT awarded him tenure a year later, but he soon started to exhibit symptoms of a serious mental illness. He experienced auditory hallucinations and claimed that aliens were sending encrypted messages to him through articles written in the *New York Times*. In April 1959 his wife committed him to McLean Hospital, a private psychiatric institution outside Boston, where doctors diagnosed him as paranoid schizophrenic. When he was released from the hospital two months later, he resigned his position at MIT, left his wife and their newborn son, John Charles Martin Nash, and traveled to Europe, where he attempted to renounce his U.S. citizenship. After reuniting with his family and moving to Princeton, he spent several months at Trenton State Hospital in New Jersey, where he was treated with insulin shock therapy.

During a period of remission Nash's colleagues obtained money from the National Science Foundation to provide him with an appointment at the IAS for the academic year 1961–62. Returning to the topic of hydrodynamics, he extended his prior work on the use of partial differential equations to analyze fluid flow. In his 1962 paper "Le problème de Cauchy pour les équations differentielles d'un fluide general" (Cauchy's problem for the differential equations of a general fluid) published in the *Bulletin de la Société Mathematique de France* (Bulletin of the Society of Mathematics of France), he proved the existence and uniqueness of solutions to a problem that French mathematician Augustin-Louis Cauchy had formulated in the 19th century. His work enabled other researchers to develop related results on the general Navier-Stokes equations in partial differential equations.

In the mid-1960s Nash experienced two more periods of mathematical productivity after extended stays in sanatoriums. In 1963, after his wife filed for divorce, he spent five months at the Carrier Clinic in Belle Meade, New Jersey, where doctors treated him with the antipsychotic drug thorazine. While at the IAS for the 1963–64 academic year, he developed a technique to resolve singularities on surfaces. Japanese mathematician Heisuke Hironaka named the technique the "Nash blowing up transformation" when he described the method in his 1983 book *Arithmetic and Geometry II*. After an eight-month stay at the Carrier Clinic in 1965, he worked for two years as a research associate at Brandeis University in Waltham, Massachusetts. In 1966 the *Annals of Mathematics* published his paper "Analyticity of Solutions of Implicit Function Problems with Analytic Data" in which he extended his previous work on the isometric imbedding theorem. During the same year he wrote another paper titled "Arc Structure of Singularities" that remained unpublished until 1995, when the *Duke Journal of Mathematics* published it in a special issue dedicated to his lifetime of work.

During the 1970s and 1980s Nash became known as the "Phantom of Fine Hall," a solitary figure who wandered through the mathematics building on Princeton's campus and scribbled cryptic messages on blackboards during the night. Living at his ex-wife's house, he spent his time working on independent projects at Princeton's library and computer center. Although most of his work during the 1970s was unproductive, he eventually developed computer programs to calculate the exact values of large numerical quantities. In the early 1990s Nash made a gradual recovery from his mental illness and returned to teaching on a limited basis.

Awarded the Nobel Prize

Many organizations have recognized the significance of Nash's work. In 1978 the Institute for Operations Research and Management Science awarded him their John von Neumann Theory Prize for his introduction of Nash equilibrium in noncooperative games. The Econometric Society elected him a fellow in 1990, the American Academy of Arts and Sciences elected him a fellow in 1995, and the National Academy of Sciences inducted him as a member in 1996. The American Mathematical Society awarded him the 1999 Leroy P. Steele Prize for Seminal Contribution to Research for his paper

"The Embedding Problem for Riemannian Manifolds." In 1994, with Hungarian economist John C. Harsanyi and German mathematician Reinhard Selten, he was named as cowinner of the Nobel Prize in economic sciences for his pioneering work in game theory.

During the past 10 years Nash has returned to his work as a mathematician. In August 1996 he described his struggles with mental illness in the plenary lecture at the 10th World Congress of Psychiatry in Madrid, Spain. The following year he published a collection of seven of his articles on game theory in the book *Essays on Game Theory*. In 2001 he remarried his ex-wife, who had helped him recover from his illness, and the movie *A Beautiful Mind* presented a biographical portrait of his life. Nash holds a position on Princeton's faculty as a senior research mathematician and continues to pursue research in mathematical logic, game theory, cosmology, and gravitation. He lectured at Pennsylvania State University in 2003 on the topics of ideal money, space-time and gravitational waves, and noncooperative games.

Conclusion

During an intensive 10-year period from 1948 to 1958, John Nash made fundamental contributions to game theory, algebraic geometry, and hydrodynamics. His introduction of the concepts of Nash equilibrium, the Nash bargaining solution, and the Nash program revolutionized the study of cooperative and noncooperative games. The Nash-Moser theorem for isometric imbeddings of manifolds solved an important problem in algebraic geometry. His work on fluid dynamics introduced new techniques in the theory of partial differential equations. After recovering from a 30-year struggle with mental illness, he was awarded the Nobel Prize in economics.

FURTHER READING

"The Bank of Sweden Prize in Economic Sciences in Memory of Alfred Nobel 1994." Nobelprize.org. URL: http://nobelprize. org/economics/laureates/1994/nash-or.html. Accessed October 19, 2005. Resources at the Nobel Prize Web site, including Nash's autobiography, a 29-minute video interview with Nash, and the transcript of a seminar titled "The Work of John Nash in Game Theory."

A Beautiful Mind. DVD and VHS, Universal Studios and DreamWorks, 2001. Oscar-winning 132-minute film reenacting significant events in Nash's life.

"A Brilliant Madness." American Experience, Public Broadcasting Service. Available online. URL: http://www.pbs.org/wgbh/amex/nash. Accessed October 19, 2005. Online resources to accompany the PBS television production "A Brilliant Madness" about Nash's work, Nobel Prize, and struggles with mental health.

Bronson, Tammy J. "John Forbes Nash, 1928– , American Algebraist and Game Theorist." In *Notable Mathematicians: From Ancient Times to the Present,* edited by Robyn V. Young, 363–364. Detroit, Mich.: Gale, 1998. Brief but informative profile of Nash and his work.

Milnor, John. "John Nash and 'A Beautiful Mind.'" *Notices of the American Mathematical Society* 45, no. 10 (November 1998): 1,329–1,332. A brief biographical profile of Nash with a summary of his work in game theory.

———. "A Nobel Prize for John Nash." *Mathematical Intelligencer* 17, no. 3 (1995): 11–17. A brief description of Nash's life and his work in game theory.

Nasar, Sylvia. *A Beautiful Mind: The Life of Mathematical Genius and Nobel Laureate John Nash.* New York: Simon and Schuster, 1998. Detailed biography that formed the basis of the motion picture.

Nash, John. *Essays on Game Theory.* Cheltenham, U.K.: Edward Elgar Publishing, 1997. A collection of seven of Nash's papers on game theory.

———. *The Essential John Nash.* Princeton, N.J.: Princeton University Press, 2001. A collection of nine of Nash's papers on game theory and manifolds, plus his autobiographical sketch written for the Nobel Prize committee.

O'Connor, J. J., and E. F. Robertson. "John Forbes Nash." MacTutor History of Mathematics Archive, University of Saint Andrews. Available online. URL: http://www-groups.dcs.st-andrews.ac.uk/~history/Mathematicians/Nash.html. Accessed January 27, 2003. Biography provided by the University of Saint Andrews, Scotland.

John H. Conway

(1937–)

John H. Conway introduced new ideas into the mathematical analysis of games, the theory of numbers, and the classification of finite groups. *(Robert Matthews)*

Inventor of the Game of Life

John Conway's creation of the Game of Life introduced a wide audience to the concept of cellular automata and to the mathematical analysis of games. His concept of surreal numbers changed mathematicians' understanding of numbers and games. The Conway group and his atlas of finite groups answered long-standing questions in group theory. His numerous books and papers made significant contributions to the study of sphere packings, lattices, codes, knots, and numerous other areas of mathematics.

Geometrical Puzzles and Finite Groups

John Horton Conway was born on December 26, 1937, in Liverpool, England, to Cyril Horton Conway and Agnes Boyce Conway. His father, who worked as a laboratory assistant at the Liverpool Institute for Boys, introduced Conway and his two older sisters to scientific and mathematical ideas at an early age. By the time he was four years old, he could mentally perform arithmetical computations such as calculating the integer powers of two: $2^1 = 2$, $2^2 = 4$, $2^3 = 8$, $2^4 = 16$, and so on. He excelled in elementary school, where he was one of the top students in most subjects. At the age of 11, Conway announced that his career goal was to become a mathematics professor at Cambridge University. In secondary school he was the best student in his mathematics classes and developed interests in astronomy, spiders, and fossils.

After completing his high school education, Conway became a scholarship student at Gonville and Caius College of Cambridge University, where he earned a bachelor's degree in mathematics in 1959. He continued his studies at Cambridge, conducting graduate-level research under the direction of number theorist Harold Davenport. For his doctoral dissertation he solved an open problem from classic number theory by proving that every positive integer can be written as the sum of 37 integers, each raised to their fifth power. While in graduate school, he became interested in mathematical logic and the properties of transfinite numbers, or numbers that specify different degrees of infinity. In 1960 he won the college's Brown Prize for Pure Mathematics. He received his doctoral degree two years later and accepted an appointment as a lecturer in pure mathematics at Cambridge.

During his years as a student at Cambridge and in the early portion of his professional career, Conway pursued his deep interest in geometrical puzzles and relationships. In 1961 he and fellow student Michael Guy mathematically analyzed the Soma cube, a three-dimensional puzzle introduced by Danish inventor Piet Hein. They determined all 240 ways to combine the seven irregular shapes to form a $3 \times 3 \times 3$ cube. Conway later invented a larger variation known as the Conway puzzle whose 18 pieces formed a $5 \times 5 \times 5$ cube. In his 1964 paper "Mrs. Perkin's Quilt," which was published in the *Proceedings of the Cambridge Philosophical*

Society, he presented an investigation of the minimum number of squares of assorted sizes that would cover an $n \times n$ square with no gaps and no overlapping areas. Throughout his career he wrote a number of articles about similar tiling, tessellation, and covering problems. He and Guy also investigated four-dimensional geometrical shapes known as polytopes or polychora. In a paper titled "Four-Dimensional Archimedean Polytopes" that he presented at the 1965 Colloquium on Convexity in Copenhagen, Denmark, he presented their enumeration of the 64 convex, nonprismatic, uniform polychora, including a new shape they discovered called the Grand Antiprism.

Conway developed new ideas and introduced an innovative notation in knot theory, the mathematical study of the properties of knots. While in high school he had investigated tangles, the fundamental two-dimensional components of knots. In his 1967 paper titled "An Enumeration of Knots and Links, and Some of Their Algebraic Properties," published in *Computational Problems in Abstract Algebra*, he introduced the Conway knot notation that provided a concise method for identifying knots in terms of their tangles. He also introduced Conway's knot—a new knot with 11 crossings that could not be produced from a combination of simpler knots—and the Conway polynomial—a polynomial whose algebraic properties corresponded to the geometric properties of the associated knot.

In the late 1960s Conway's analysis of a massive geometrical structure led to the discovery of three new objects and the solution of a classic problem in group theory, the branch of algebra concerned with the analysis of mathematical structures. In 1965 English mathematician John Leech had found a way to pack hyperspheres in 24 dimensions so that each object touched 196,560 others. During a single 12-hour research session Conway completely analyzed the mathematical properties of this Leech lattice. He announced his discovery in a 1968 article titled "A Perfect Group of Order 8,315,553,613,086,720,000 and the Sporadic Simple Groups" that was published in the *Proceedings of the National Academy of Science, USA* and provided a fuller description of the group in his 1969 paper "A Group of Order 8,315,553,613,086,720,000," which appeared in the *Bulletin of the London Mathematical Society*. In his research Conway provided the details of a massive group that contained within itself the structures of almost all of the then-known finite, sporadic simple groups. He showed that the structure also contained three previously unknown groups now known as the Conway groups: Co_1, having 4,157,776,806,543,360,000 elements; Co_2, having 42,305,421,312,000 elements; and Co_3, having 495,766,656,000 elements.

During the next 15 years Conway and four of his former doctoral students from Cambridge University, Robert T. Curtis, Simon P. Norton, Richard A. Parker, and Robert A. Wilson compiled a complete listing of all finite groups, a problem that algebraists had been trying to solve for more than a century. Their 1985 book *Atlas of Finite Groups: Maximal Subgroups and Ordinary Characters for Simple Groups* presented a comprehensive categorization of all finite groups—sets with finitely many elements that satisfy four algebraic properties—and a detailed description of their structures. During the intervening years Conway produced numerous papers discussing specific groups, including his 1979 paper with Norton, "Monstrous Moonshine," which appeared in the *Bulletin of the London Mathematical Society.* In this paper they analyzed the monster group that has more than 8×10^{53} elements and proposed the moonshine conjecture relating the monster group with the theory of elliptic functions, a conjecture whose solution earned English mathematician Richard Borcherds the 1998 Fields Medal.

The Game of Life

The mathematics of games and the invention of new games became a hobby and a topic of research for Conway. In the 1960s he and Cambridge University colleague Michael S. Patterson invented the game Sprouts, a two-person game played with pencil and paper. Starting with two dots on a piece of paper, players take turns joining any two dots with a curve that does not cross any curve already drawn and then add a new dot somewhere on the new curve. The game ends when one player cannot draw a curve joining two dots without crossing another curve or connecting to a dot that already is connected to three dots. Conway later introduced a modified version of this game known as Sprouts that used crosses instead of dots and allowed four edges to meet at each cross.

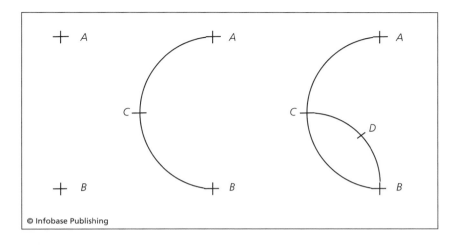

© Infobase Publishing

One of the pencil and paper games Conway invented was Sprouts. Starting with two crosses, *A* and *B*, a possible move for the first player is to join one arm of each cross and add a new crossbar at *C*. The second player might choose to connect an arm of *C* to an arm of *B* and add a new crossbar at *D*. The game continues until one player cannot connect two arms without crossing an existing curve.

Two other games that Conway invented and analyzed were Phutball and Sylver Coinage. Philosopher's Football, or Phutball, is a two-person game played with black and white markers on a square grid such as a Go board. After a black marker representing the ball is placed at the center of the board, the players take turns placing a white stone on the board or jumping the ball over one or more white stones in an attempt to move the ball past the goal line at the opponent's edge of the board. In the 1970s Conway created the numbers game Sylver Coinage in which two players take turns naming a positive integer as the value of a new coin that represents a monetary amount that cannot be generated by any combination of previously introduced coins. British-born Canadian mathematician Richard Guy's article "Twenty Questions Concerning Conway's Sylver Coinage," which appeared in 1976 in the *American Mathematical Monthly* discussed the mathematical aspects of this game.

In 1970 Conway invented his most widely known game, the Game of Life. In it, each cell on a square grid is designated as either alive or dead. In successive time steps, or generations, each live cell survives or dies and each dead cell remains dead or springs to life based on the status of their eight neighboring cells. A live cell with fewer than two neighbors dies of isolation in the next generation, while a live cell with more than three neighbors dies of overcrowding. A dead cell having exactly three neighbors comes to life in the next time step.

With this simple set of rules known as "23/3," Conway discovered configurations of cells that grew, reproduced, and interacted with their environment. He found many configurations of cells that produced recurring patterns or converged to a fixed pattern with the passage of time. A row or column of three cells that he called

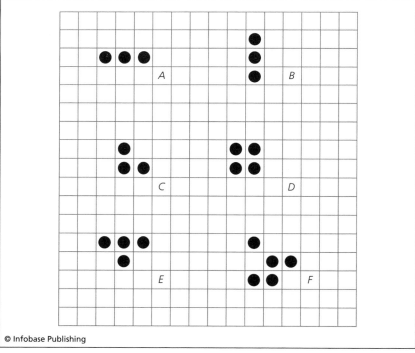

© Infobase Publishing

In Conway's Game of Life, a row of three cells (A) or a column of three cells (B) form blinkers that alternate horizontally and vertically from one generation to the next. An L–shaped group of three cells (C) becomes a 2 x 2 block of cells (D) that remains fixed. A T-shaped pattern of four cells (E) stabilizes to form a set of four blinkers after nine generations. Five cells arranged into a pattern known as a glider (F) move one space diagonally every four generations.

blinkers alternated horizontally and vertically from one generation to the next. An L-shaped group of three cells became a 2 × 2 block of cells that remained fixed. A T-shaped pattern of four cells stabilized to form a set of four blinkers after nine generations. Five cells arranged into a pattern known as a glider moved one space diagonally every four generations.

Mathematics writer Martin Gardner publicized Conway's Game of Life in a series of 10 installments in his "Mathematical Games" column in *Scientific American* magazine between October 1970 and December 1975. An instant success, Life introduced a wide audience to the concept of cellular automata, the generation of patterns on grids of cells according to rules concerning the status of a cell and its neighbors. Amateur and professional mathematicians implemented Life on computers to analyze a variety of initial configurations. When Conway challenged the readers of Gardner's column to create a self-perpetuating life-form, William Gosper at the Massachusetts Institute of Technology's Artificial Intelligence Laboratory discovered the glider gun that produced and ejected an unending series of gliders. Scientific researchers have used Life and other forms of cellular automata to model the role of DNA in carrying information between generations of living organisms and to investigate questions about the process of evolution and natural selection.

Conway's interest in the mathematical analysis of games led him to develop a new category of numbers that became known as surreal numbers. While analyzing the game Go in the early 1970s, he observed that the last portion of each contest consisted of a collection of smaller games whose combinations shared many properties with numbers. Pursuing this observation, he developed an expanded concept of number in which every two-person game is a number. His surreal numbers form a natural completion of the number system containing the integers, rationals, reals, complex, and transfinite numbers. American computer scientist Donald Knuth introduced the term *surreal* in his 1974 novel *Surreal Numbers: How Two Ex-Students Turned on to Pure Mathematics and Found Total Happiness*, a work of fiction that portrayed Conway in the role of God.

Conway wrote three books about games, their analysis, and their relation to numbers. In his 1975 book, *All Games Bright and*

Beautiful, he presented his formal analyses of a large collection of games, including some of the games he invented. His 1976 work, *On Numbers and Games*, or *ONAG* as the book has become known, explained the relationship between surreal numbers and the mathematical analysis of games. In 1982, with fellow mathematicians Richard Guy and Elwyn Berlekamp, he coauthored a two-volume work titled *Winning Ways for Your Mathematical Plays*, which presented the sophisticated mathematical analysis of hundreds of games of strategy. In chapter 25 of this work, they proved that the Game of Life is a universal Turing machine, meaning that it can be used as a computer to answer any question that can be answered using mathematics.

His work with geometrical puzzles, knot theory, finite groups, and the theory of games earned Conway recognition within the mathematical community. He was elected a fellow at Cambridge University's Sidney Sussex College in 1964 and at Gonville and Caius College in 1970. The London Mathematical Society awarded him their 1971 Berwick Prize for his work on finite groups. In 1975 Gardner dedicated his book *Mathematical Carnival* to Conway for his contributions to recreational mathematics. That same year Cambridge promoted him from lecturer to reader in pure mathematics and mathematical statistics, a position he held until 1983 when they promoted him to the rank of professor. He received his country's highest academic honor in 1981 when he was elected a fellow of the Royal Society of London.

Analysis of Numbers

In addition to puzzles, games, groups, and knots, Conway made many discoveries about numbers and number sequences. He published some of his early observations of numerical properties in his 1972 book *All Numbers Great and Small*. In his 1973 paper "Tomorrow Is the Day after Doomsday," published in the journal *Eureka*, he explained his Doomsday algorithm that enabled him to calculate mentally the day of the week for any given date in the past or the future within two seconds. Using a similar method, he was able to determine the phase of the Moon in a similar amount of time.

Conway developed an algorithm for generating the entire sequence of prime numbers using only the operation of multiplying fractions. He presented his technique in 1980 as "Problem 2.4" in the journal *Mathematical Intelligencer* and challenged readers to analyze his method. His prime producing machine consisted of a list of 14 fractions lettered *A* through *N*. Starting with the number 2, one multiplied the current number by the first listed fraction that generated an integer result. One repeated this process until the answer was a power of two. The exponent in this expression was the next prime number, and the process of multiplication continued. This simple but inefficient algorithm required 280 steps to produce the first three prime numbers, 2, 3, and 5.

In his 1986 paper "The Weird and Wonderful Chemistry of Audioactive Decay," which was published in the journal *Eureka*, Conway introduced the look and say sequence and presented a thorough analysis of its properties. Beginning with the digit 1, each subsequent term of the sequence is generated by reading the number of consecutive occurrences of each distinct digit in the current term. By this rule the second term is "one 1" which is written 11; the third term is "two 1s" and is written 21; the fourth term is "one 2 one 1" or 1211. The next few terms are 111221, 312211, and 13112221. In his paper Conway proved that the number of digits in the *n*th term of the sequence was proportional to λ^n, where λ is the Conway constant whose value of approximately 1.303577 is the only positive root of a particular polynomial of degree 71.

$\frac{17}{91}$	$\frac{78}{85}$	$\frac{19}{51}$	$\frac{23}{38}$	$\frac{29}{33}$	$\frac{77}{29}$	$\frac{95}{23}$	$\frac{77}{19}$	$\frac{1}{17}$	$\frac{11}{13}$	$\frac{13}{11}$	$\frac{15}{14}$	$\frac{15}{2}$	$\frac{55}{1}$
A	B	C	D	E	F	G	H	I	J	K	L	M	N

© Infobase Publishing

Conway created this sequence of 14 fractions that form an inefficient but simple-minded prime-producing machine. Starting with the number 2, repeatedly multiply the current value by the first fraction in the list that produces an integer result. When the answer is a power of 2, the exponent is the next prime number. The first 19 steps produce $2M = 15$, $15N = 825$, $825E = 725$, . . . , $68I = 4 = 2^2$, so 2 is the first prime number. After 50 more steps one obtains $8 = 2^3$ to conclude that 3 is the second prime number.

During the lecture "Some Crazy Sequences" that he delivered in 1988 at AT&T Bell Labs, Conway introduced the recursively defined sequence whose first two terms are $A(1) = 1$, $A(2) = 1$ and whose nth term is defined by the expression $A(n) = A(A(n-1)) + A(n - A(n-1))$. The first several terms of this sequence, known as Conway's recursive sequence, are $1,1,2,2,3,4,4,4,5,6,7,8, \ldots$ He showed that $A(2^k) = 2^{k-1}$ for any positive integer k, $A(2n) \le 2 \cdot A(n)$ for any positive integer n, and for large values of n, the general term of the sequence is very close to $\frac{n}{2}$. He offered a $1,000 prize to anyone who could find an integer N so that $\left| \frac{A_n}{n} - \frac{1}{2} \right| < \frac{1}{20}$ whenever $n > N$. In 1991 Bell Labs researcher Colin L. Mallows proved that $N = 1,489$ had the required property and claimed the monetary prize.

During the last 10 years Conway has written two books about numbers and their properties. *The Book of Numbers*, which he coauthored in 1996 with Richard Guy, presents an array of ideas about numbers, including properties of classes of numbers such as integers, fractions, and surreal numbers; important results from number theory; and properties of special numbers such as $\pi \approx 3.14159$. Pointing out the inconsistent usage of terms such as *billion* and *trillion*, the book introduced the term *Nth zillion* for the number 1 followed by $3N + 3$ zeros in the United States and $6N$ zeros in Great Britain. The 2003 book *On Quaternions and Octonions: Their Geometry, Arithmetic, and Symmetry* that he cowrote with his former student Derek Smith presents an investigation of the four- and eight-dimensional geometries that can be analyzed using the classes of numbers known as quaternions and octonions.

Spheres, Lattices, and Codes

Conway completed much of his work on numbers in the United States. He left Cambridge in 1984 to accept a temporary appointment as the Rademacher Lecturer at the University of Pennsylvania. After spending the fall semester of 1985 as a visiting professor at the University of Illinois at Chicago, he accepted a permanent position as the John von Neumann Chair of Mathematics at Princeton

University in New Jersey. At Princeton he has continued to generate papers and books on a collection of related topics, including sphere packing, integral lattices, and coding theory.

In 1988 Conway and American mathematician Neil J. H. Sloane coauthored the book *Sphere Packing, Lattices, and Groups*, which presented a survey of recent research results in combinatorics, the study of counting techniques. Other mathematicians who analyze the geometry of sphere packing—the most efficient arrangement of equal-sized spheres into a space having a fixed volume—refer to this book as the "bible" on the subject. Between 1988 and 1997 Conway and Sloane cowrote a series of seven papers about algebraic structures known as lattices, sets of points laid out in a regular, repeating pattern in a multidimensional space. In their articles, collectively titled "Low-Dimensional Lattices," which were published in the *Proceedings of the Royal Society of London*, they explored quadratic forms, perfect forms, groups of matrices, and issues involving coordinates. The two are currently working on a book tentatively titled *The Geometry of Low-Dimensional Groups and Lattices*.

Conway has also produced research results in the related area of coding theory, the analysis of methods for manipulating and transmitting blocks of data. His work on this topic dates back to the late 1970s when he wrote papers on self-dual binary codes. In 1985 he and Sloane received a patent for "Decoding Techniques for Multi-Dimensional Codes." His more recent work includes the 1990 paper "Integral Lexicographic Codes," published in the journal *Discrete Mathematics*; the 1993 paper "Self-Dual Codes over the Integers Modulo 4," published in the *Journal of Combinatorial Theory*; and the 1994 paper "Sphere Packings, Lattices, Codes and Greed," which appeared in the *Proceedings of the International Congress of Mathematicians*.

Three papers written in the last 15 years typify the diversity of Conway's interests. In his 1992 paper "The Orbifold Notation for Surface Groups," published in the conference proceedings *Groups, Combinatorics and Geometry*, he introduced a simple way to enumerate crystallographic, spherical, and wallpaper groups, three types of algebraic structures that satisfy additional geometric properties. His 1996 paper "The Angel Problem," which appeared in *Games of No Chance*, challenged readers to determine whether a devil who can remove one square at a time from an infinite-sized chess board can capture an angel capable of jumping up to 1,000 squares at a time. In 2004 Conway and his Princeton colleague Simon Kochen proved the free will theorem, a result from quantum mechanics stating that under certain conditions elementary particles are free to choose their spins. Both mathematicians have lectured widely on their controversial result but have not yet published their proof.

Since joining the faculty at Princeton, Conway has continued to earn awards and honors similar to those that he received while at Cambridge. In 1987 the London Mathematical Society awarded him their Pólya Prize for creativity and imaginative expository writing. That same year the Institute for Electrical and Electronics Engineers (IEEE) presented him and Sloane an award for outstanding paper of the year for their 1986 paper "Lexicographic Codes: Error-Correcting Codes from Game Theory," which appeared in the *IEEE Transactions on Information Theory*. In 1991 Conway delivered the Earle Raymond Hedrick Lectures at the Joint Summer Meetings of the American Mathematical Society (AMS) and the Mathematical Association of America, a set of lectures that formed the basis for his 1997 book *The Sensual (Quadratic) Form*. The American Academy of Arts and Sciences elected him a fellow in 1992. He received the 1998 Frederic Esser Nemmers Prize in Mathematics from Northwestern University for having made major contributions to new knowledge. In 2000 the AMS named him the recipient of the Leroy P. Steele Prize for Mathematical Exposition in recognition of his expository contributions to many branches of mathematics.

Conclusion

During a career that has spanned five decades, John H. Conway has written 10 books, published approximately 150 research papers, and directed the dissertation research of 13 doctoral students. His creation of the Game of Life exposed a broad audience to the study of cellular automata and mathematical games. Through his introduction of surreal numbers he redefined mathematicians' understanding of numbers and games. His discovery of the Conway group and his work to complete the classification of finite groups resolved important open questions in group theory. By raising questions and by writing books and papers, he has made significant contributions to the study of sphere packings, lattices, codes, knots, and numerous other areas of mathematics.

FURTHER READING

Albers, Don. "John Horton Conway—Talking a Good Game." *Math Horizons*, Spring 1994, pp. 6–9. Brief article about Conway and some of his discoveries.

Conway, John H., and Derek A. Smith. *On Quaternions and Octonions: Their Geometry, Arithmetic, and Symmetry.* Natick, Mass.: Peters, 2003. Presents the mathematics of these four- and eight-dimensional number groups; for mathematically sophisticated audiences.

Conway, John H., and Richard K. Guy. *The Book of Numbers.* New York: Springer, 1996. One of Conway's books for general audiences presenting both simple and advanced concepts about numbers.

Gardner, Martin. "Mathematical Games. The Fantastic Combinations of John Conway's New Solitaire Game 'Life.'" *Scientific American* 223, no. 10 (1970): 120–123. The first of Gardner's 10 articles that described and popularized the Game of Life.

Guy, Richard K. "John Horton Conway." In *Mathematical People: Profiles and Interviews*, edited by Donald J. Albers and Gerald L. Alexanderson, 42–50. Boston: Birkhauser, 1985. A description of 10 of Conway's discoveries, mostly in recreational games. Reprint of 1982 article from *The Two-Year College Mathematics Journal.*

Henderson, Harry. "John H. Conway (1937–)." In *Modern Mathematicians*, 122–132. New York: Facts On File, 1996. Profile of Conway with particular attention to the Game of Life.

"John Conway." Wikipedia, the Free Encyclopedia. Available online. URL: http://en.wikipedia.org/wiki/John_H_Conway. Accessed October 26, 2005. Brief biography with links to other sites and additional explanations.

O'Connor, J. J., and E. F. Robertson. "John Horton Conway." MacTutor History of Mathematics Archive, University of Saint

Andrews. Available online. URL: http://www-groups.dcs.st-andrews.ac.uk/~history/Mathematicians/Conway.html. Accessed November 4, 2005. Biography provided by the University of Saint Andrews, Scotland.

Seife, Charles. "Mathemagician." *Sciences*, May/June 1994, pp. 12–15. Interview with Conway focusing on the Game of Life and other recreational activities.

Weisstein, Eric. "Life." Mathworld—A Wolfram Web Resource. Available online. URL: http://mathworld.wolfram.com/Life.html. Accessed October 25, 2005. Article explaining Conway's Game of Life.

5

Stephen Hawking

(1942–   )

Stephen Hawking developed the mathematical basis for the theory of black holes. (*Michael S. Yamashita/ CORBIS*)

The Mathematics of Black Holes

Stephen Hawking helped develop topological and geometrical tools that enabled him to show that the big bang theory was consistent with the principles of general relativity. He discovered a mathematical proof that Hawking radiation escapes from black holes and can cause them to collapse and evaporate. In his position as Cambridge University's Lucasian Professor of Mathematics, he introduced the controversial "no-boundary" proposal and the "information paradox."

As a popular science writer, he authored books on cosmology that have made advanced scientific ideas accessible to nonspecialists.

Early Life and Education

Stephen William Hawking was born on January 8, 1942, in Oxford, England, to Frank Hawking, a medical researcher specializing in tropical diseases, and Isobel Hawking, the daughter of a physician. His parents, both of whom had graduated from University College at Oxford University, provided an intellectually stimulating environment for Hawking and his three younger siblings, Mary, Philippa, and Edward. After his father became head of the division of parasitology at the National Institute of Medical Research in Mill Hill in the late 1940s, the family moved from Highgate, a northern suburb of London, to St. Albans in Hertfordshire to be closer to their father's work.

From 1952 to 1959 Hawking attended St. Albans School where he placed in the highest of the school's three academic tracks. He demonstrated insight and natural ability for mathematics, mastering his coursework in the subject with minimal effort. He also developed an interest in chemistry and wrote a prize-winning paper in theology. In 1958, with his fellow students and their mathematics teacher, he helped design and build a primitive computer called the Logical Uniselector Computing Machine (LUCE). Outside school he enjoyed constructing model airplanes, building electronic devices, and inventing board games that incorporated highly developed characters and intricate rules.

In 1959 Hawking won a scholarship to attend Oxford's University College. Although his father wanted him to study medicine and biology, he enrolled as a student in the natural sciences with specializations in physics and mathematics. During his first year he attended only mathematics lectures and tutorials and completed his college examinations in that subject. At the end of his second year he won the University Physics Prize and received a Blackwell Book Award for excellence in physics. He participated in intercollegiate rowing competitions as a coxswain with one of the university's crew teams. In 1962 he graduated with honors, earning a bachelor of arts degree in natural sciences, first class.

After leaving Oxford, Hawking spent four years as a graduate student in the Department of Applied Mathematics and Theoretical Physics at Cambridge University, where he conducted research in cosmology and general relativity under the direction of professor Dennis Sciama. Cosmology, the study of the origin and evolution of the universe, is a highly mathematical branch of physics. The general theory of relativity, invented in the early 20th century by German-born physicist Albert Einstein, explains the laws of gravity and the behavior of the universe at large. Quantum theory, another branch of physics, explains the properties of atoms, molecules, light, and the radiation of small particles. When Hawking entered graduate school, relativity and quantum theory were prominent but separate branches of modern physics that along with classical physics, formulated by Sir Isaac Newton and his contemporaries, constituted the basis of his physics curriculum.

In January 1963, after experiencing difficulty speaking and walking, Hawking underwent two weeks of medical tests. Doctors diagnosed him with motor neuron disease, a degenerative disorder of the muscular system also known as amyotrophic lateral sclerosis (ALS) or Lou Gehrig's disease. His physicians explained that his physical condition would cause his body, but not his mind, to deteriorate quickly and estimated that he would die within two-and-a-half years.

Hawking refused to allow his medical condition to prevent him from pursuing his personal and professional interests. In July 1965 he married Jane Wilde, an undergraduate pursuing a degree in modern languages at Westfield College in London and who later earned a doctorate in medieval Portuguese literature. Between 1967 and 1979 the couple had three children, Robert, Lucy, and Timothy. Although Hawking was confined to a wheelchair within five years and his ability to speak deteriorated progressively, he was able to commute daily to the university from their rented house near Cambridge's campus.

Investigations of Black Holes

Hawking rapidly became an active member of the research community of cosmologists. At a 1965 meeting of the Royal Society in

London, he challenged an assertion made by Cambridge astronomy professor Sir Fred Hoyle and his graduate student Jayant Narlikar during their presentation on the theory of a steady-state universe. Hawking observed that a mathematical quantity in one of their equations diverged rather than adding up to a finite total. He summarized the mathematical findings that led him to this conclusion in a paper titled "On the Hoyle-Narlikar Theory of Gravitation," published later that year in the *Proceedings of the Royal Society of London*. This article was well received by his peers and established his reputation as a promising young researcher.

In 1966 Hawking earned his Ph.D. in physics for a dissertation titled "Occurrence of Singularities in Cosmology," which was published during the next year in three parts in the *Proceedings of the Royal Society of London*. His doctoral research built on the work of Roger Penrose, a professor of applied mathematics at Birkbeck College, London, who had been investigating black holes. American physicist John Wheeler introduced the term *black hole* to describe a dense concentration of mass so great that its gravitational field prevents any mass or energy, including light, from escaping. Penrose had developed a mathematical theory to explain space-time singularities at the center of a black hole, points where the curvature of space-time is infinite. In his dissertation Hawking applied Penrose's ideas of singularity theory to the universe as a whole. His unpublished essay "Singularities and the Geometry of Space-Time" that presented a continuation of his thesis work won the 1966 Adams Prize from Cambridge University.

After receiving his doctoral degree, Hawking secured a two-year appointment as a research fellow in theoretical physics at Cambridge's Gonville and Caius College and in 1968 joined the staff at the university's Institute of Astronomy. He and Penrose worked to investigate further their joint ideas about singularities and the origin of the universe. They developed an extensive set of topological and geometrical tools, now known as global methods, for making general relativity calculations. In their joint work they showed that if the general theory of relativity provided an accurate description of the universe, then there must have been a singularity at the beginning of time. The Hawking-Penrose theorem mathematically proved the big bang theory that the universe began with the explosion of a black hole. Their 1970 paper explaining this work, "The Singularities of Gravitational Collapse and Cosmology," which appeared in the *Proceedings of the Royal Society of London* made a major contribution to black hole theory.

In the course of developing his theories about black holes, Hawking published some incomplete ideas that he later disproved. One of these topics concerned his initial analysis of the event horizon, the boundary of a black hole beyond which no electromagnetic energy can travel. His paper "Gravitational Radiation from Colliding Black Holes" that was published in 1971 in *Physical Review Letters* presented his claim that the surface area of a black hole's event horizon can never decrease. In a 1973 paper titled "The Four Laws of Black Hole Mechanics" that appeared in *Communications in Mathematical Physics*, he and coauthors James Bardeen, an American physicist, and Brandon Carter, a British theoretical physicist, attempted to explain why black holes were not subject to the laws of thermodynamics, or the study of heat and motion. Within two years Hawking had abandoned both positions and used the opposing ideas to develop additional theories.

Hawking left the Institute of Astronomy in 1973 to join the research staff at Cambridge's Department of Applied Mathematics and Theoretical Physics. That same year, after six years of work, he and George Ellis, a South African cosmologist, completed their book *The Large-Scale Structure of Space-Time*. Although the work presented classical theories of cosmology for an audience of experts and did not include recently developed theories on black holes, the book sold more than 16,000 copies and became one of the best-selling monographs published by Cambridge University Press.

Hawking Radiation and the Information Paradox

Reconsidering some of his earlier claims about black holes, Hawking applied the principles of quantum theory, general relativity, and thermodynamics to their study. Combining all three techniques, he succeeded in proving the surprising result that black holes emit a type of radiation now known as Hawking radiation. This discovery contradicted his earlier belief that the surface area of a black hole's event horizon could never decrease and meant that the escaping mass and energy could eventually cause a black hole to shrink and

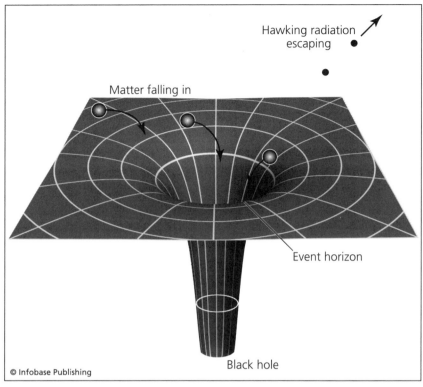

Matter falling in

Hawking radiation escaping

Event horizon

© Infobase Publishing

Black hole

The dense concentration of mass in a black hole is so great that its gravitational field prevents any mass or energy, including light, from escaping beyond its event horizon and creates a curvature in space-time. Using the principles of quantum theory, general relativity, and thermodynamics, Hawking mathematically established the controversial idea that black holes emit Hawking radiation.

disappear. He announced his results in an essay titled "Black Holes Aren't Black" that won the 1974 Gravity Research Foundation Award, and he provided a more complete description of the proof in his paper "Black Hole Expansions?" that appeared later that year in the journal *Nature*. Sciama described the latter article as one of the most beautiful papers on physics ever written. In March 1974, on the basis of this discovery and his earlier work on the big bang theory, the Royal Society elected 32-year-old Hawking as a fellow.

The discovery of Hawking radiation presented physicists with an apparent contradiction known as the information paradox.

According to Hawking's theory, the radiation escaping from a black hole had "no hair," meaning that it conveyed no information about the matter inside the black hole that would distinguish it from another black hole having the same mass, electrical charge, and angular momentum. After a sufficient amount of radiation escaped from the black hole, it would collapse and the information would be lost. This paradox contradicted a fundamental principle of physics that information is preserved as the universe evolves. Hawking formulated and explored the information paradox in his 1976 paper "Breakdown of Predictability in Gravitational Collapse," published in *Physical Review D.* He supported the idea that the intense gravitational field that resulted in the collapse of a black hole constituted a singularity to which the laws of quantum physics did not apply. Other physicists criticized the controversial information paradox because it would mean that science was no longer able to fully know the past or to predict the future.

By the mid-1970s Hawking's contributions to science had earned recognition in England and abroad. He had spent the year 1974 studying cosmology at the California Institute of Technology as a Sherman Fairchild Distinguished Scholar. Upon his return to England, Cambridge University provided him a wheelchair-accessible house near the campus and appointed him a reader of gravitational physics. In 1975 the Royal Astronomical Society awarded him the Eddington Medal and the Pontifical Academy of Science presented him with the Pius XII Medal. The following year Hawking won the Hopkins Prize, the Dannie Heinemann Prize, the Maxwell Prize, and the Royal Society's Hughes Medal. In 1977 Cambridge promoted him to the rank of professor of gravitational physics, Gonville and Caius College awarded him the status of professorial fellow, and Oxford's University College made him an honorary fellow. He was awarded the 1978 Albert Einstein Award, an honor similar in prestige to the Nobel Prize.

The End of Physics and the No-Boundary Proposal

Throughout his career Hawking continued to raise controversial issues and stimulate debate within the physics community. In 1980

Cambridge University appointed him the 17th Lucasian Professor of Mathematics, a chair previously held by Sir Isaac Newton and a series of distinguished mathematicians. For his inaugural address as Lucasian Professor, he delivered a lecture titled "Is the End in Sight for Theoretical Physics?" In this talk he predicted that by the end of the 20th century physicists would discover a grand unified theory that encompassed both pillars of modern physics—quantum theory and general relativity—leaving no significant discoveries to be made. He further predicted that as computers develop more sophistication and artificial intelligence becomes a reality, advanced technology will execute most of the current activities now performed by physicists. His predictions generated lively debate among his scientific colleagues. Although his research that led to the discovery of Hawking radiation provided a model for combining both quantum mechanics and relativity, scientists have made little progress toward achieving a grand unified theory.

In 1981 Hawking generated additional controversy when he announced his "no-boundary" proposal and discussed its religious implications at the Vatican Conference organized by the Pontifical Academy of Sciences in Rome, Italy. He and American physicist James Hartle had proposed the idea that both time and space were finite in extent but had no edges or singular points where the laws of science failed to hold. In particular their proposal implied that in the range of possible universes, our universe was so highly probable that there was no need to believe in the existence of a creator. Their proposal generated strong criticism within both the religious and the scientific communities.

Popular Science for General Audiences

From the mid-1980s to the present, Hawking has devoted a significant portion of his time to writing books that make mathematical and scientific ideas accessible to nonspecialists. From 1983 to 1988 he worked on a project to explain concepts of modern cosmology, such as the big bang theory, black holes, and Hawking radiation, in a manner that general audiences could understand. The product of his five years of work was the 1988 book *A Brief History of Time: From the Big Bang to Black Holes*. The book sold 10 million copies, was translated into 40 languages, and remained on the best-seller lists of both the *New York Times* and London's *Sunday Times* for four years. The book became a movie in 1991. In 1992 he produced an accompanying book, titled *Stephen Hawking's A Brief History of Time: A Reader's Companion*, and in 1994 he released the CD-ROM version, *A Brief History of Time: An Interactive Adventure*. The 1995 paperback edition of *A Brief History of Time* became a best-seller in three days. In 2005 he produced an updated and simplified version of the work, *A Briefer History of Time*.

The unexpected popularity of *A Brief History of Time* led to numerous newspaper and magazine articles about Hawking, requests for radio and television appearances, invitations for public presentations and lectures, and proposals for additional book projects. In 1993 he edited a collection of 14 essays on cosmology titled *Black Holes and Baby Universes* that communicated current theories to an audience of educated lay readers. His 2001 book *The Universe in a Nutshell*, which offered simplified explanations of scientific ideas and was illustrated with colorful diagrams on every page, won the 2002 Aventis Book Prize, one of the United Kingdom's most prestigious nonfiction book awards. In 2002 he published the book *On the Shoulders of Giants: The Great Works of Physics and Astronomy*, which combined lengthy portions of influential works by Nicolaus Copernicus, Johannes Kepler, Galileo Galilei, Sir Isaac Newton, and Albert Einstein with biographical sketches of the five scientists and Hawking's explanations of the meaning and significance of their contributions to physics and astronomy. His 2005 book *God Created the Integers: The Mathematical Breakthroughs That Changed History* included reprints of 31 landmarks of mathematical thought, Hawking's commentary on the significance of each work, and biographical profiles of the 17 mathematicians who made these momentous discoveries.

Science for Scientists

While creating written and visual works to interest the general public in cosmology and mathematics, Hawking continued to contribute to the discussion and development of new theories in physics. In 1979 he and German-born Canadian physicist Werner Israel edited *General Relativity: An Einstein Centenary Survey*, a collection of 16 articles written by leading physicists in commemoration of the 100th anniversary of Einstein's birth. His 1983 paper "Fluctuations in the Inflationary Universe," which appeared in the journal *Nuclear Physics*, and his 1984 article "Limits on Inflationary Models of the Universe," which was published in *Physics Letters*, contributed to the discussion among his colleagues about the causes, extents, and implications of the expansion of the universe.

In August 1985, while conducting research at the European Center for Nuclear Research (CERN) in Geneva, Switzerland, Hawking contracted pneumonia. Doctors performed a tracheotomy that saved his life but deprived him of his ability to speak. American computer researchers provided him with a computer-generated voice synthesizer. This initial device and a series of subsequent upgrades provided him the ability to continue to lecture and communicate with his family members and other researchers.

Hawking's successful career as a scientist living with disabilities has enabled him to be a visible advocate for the needs of people with disabilities. In 1979 the Royal Association for Disability and Rehabilitation named him "Man of the Year." During the late 1980s he convinced Cambridge University to construct a hostel for handicapped students and persuaded Bristol University to build a dormitory for physically challenged students that they named Hawking House. In 1996 he wrote the foreword to the book *Computer Resources for People with Disabilities*.

After his surgery Hawking continued to share his ideas on current developments in physics with his colleagues. In his 1988 paper "Wormholes in Space-Time," published in *Physical Review;* his 1991 paper "Alpha Parameters of Wormholes," which appeared in *Physica Scripta;* and many additional papers that he wrote on the topic, he discussed the mathematical possibility of time travel within a single universe and between parallel universes. He engaged his colleagues in discussions on string theory, the concept that strings of matter form the fundamental building blocks of all substances. His papers on string theory include his 1989 article "Black Holes from Cosmic Strings," which appeared in *Physics Letters*, and his paper "Pair Production of Black Holes on Cosmic Strings," which was published in 1995 in *Physical Review Letters*. In 1994, at

Cambridge's Isaac Newton Institute, Hawking and Penrose gave a series of public lectures collectively titled "The Nature of Space and Time" that reviewed the developments of black hole theory since their collaboration began, 30 years earlier.

Over the past 20 years Hawking's accomplishments have earned him additional recognition and honors. In 1988 he and Penrose were jointly awarded the Wolf Foundation Prize in Physics for their work on black holes. Having already been honored by Queen Elizabeth II with the title Commander of the Order of the British Empire (CBE) in 1982, he was awarded the additional title Companion of Honour in 1989. The National Academy of Sciences of the United States inducted him as a member of the astronomy section in 1992. The London Mathematical Society awarded Hawking its 1999 Naylor Prize and Lectureship in Applied Mathematics. In January 2002 an international assemblage of 200 physicists gathered at Cambridge University to attend "The Future of Theoretical Physics and Cosmology, Stephen Hawking 60th Birthday Scientific Workshop," an international conference to celebrate his 60th birthday and to discuss the ideas he contributed to the field during his 40-year career.

After writing almost 200 books and papers and supervising the doctoral dissertations of 30 graduate students, Hawking continues to work on the frontier of cosmology. At the International Conference on General Relativity and Gravitation (GR17) held in Dublin, Ireland, in July 2004, he announced that he had resolved the information paradox by reversing his earlier position and showing that information is not lost in the formation and evaporation of a black hole. Over the course of three decades he had come to the conclusion that the event horizon of a black hole includes quantum fluctuations that gradually allow all information in the black hole to escape. He continues to work to produce a formal mathematical proof of this claim.

Conclusion

Stephen Hawking's controversial mathematical proof that black holes emit radiation and that Hawking radiation can result in their eventual collapse represented a significant contribution to

20th-century cosmology. He helped to develop topological and geometrical tools that enabled him to establish the validity of the big bang theory. As Lucasian Professor of Mathematics at Cambridge University, he engaged his colleagues in investigations of the mathematical principles underlying the no boundary proposal, the information paradox, the grand unified theory, and other developing concepts in physics. His popular books have enabled the general public to gain a greater understanding of advanced scientific ideas about cosmology.

FURTHER READING

Bruen, Robert. "Stephen Hawking." The Lucasian Chair of Mathematics at Cambridge, 1693–1993, Boston College. Available online. URL: http://www.lucasianchair.org/hawking.html. Accessed February 23, 2006. Profile of Hawking and a discussion of his work by Professor Bruen. The information presented about Hawking is part of a larger set of pages on the history of the Lucasian Chair of Mathematics.

Hawking, Stephen. *A Brief History of Time: From the Big Bang to Black Holes.* New York: Bantam, 1988. Hawking's best-selling book, also available in a film version, as a reader's companion, and on CD-ROM.

———. "Professor Stephen W. Hawking's website." Cambridge University. Available online. URL: http://www.hawking.org.uk/home/hindex.html. Accessed October 27, 2005. University-sponsored Web site about Hawking, his research, his lectures, and his disabilities.

Hawking, Stephen, ed. *God Created the Integers: The Mathematical Breakthroughs That Changed History.* Philadelphia: Running Press, 2005. Presents reprints of 31 landmarks of mathematical thought from 17 influential mathematicians, along with Hawking's commentary on their significance and biographical profiles of each individual.

Kramer, Jennifer. "Stephen W. Hawking, 1942– , English Cosmological Physicist." In *Notable Mathematicians: From Ancient Times to the Present*, edited by Robyn V. Young, 233–235. Detroit, Mich.: Gale, 1998. Brief profile of Hawking and his work.

Mailet, Hélène. "Is the End in Sight for the Lucasian Chair? Stephen Hawking as Millennium Professor." In *From Newton to Hawking: A History of Cambridge University's Lucasian Professor of Mathematics*, edited by Kevin C. Knox and Richard Noakes, 425–459. Cambridge: Cambridge University Press, 2003. An essay incorporating a partial biographical sketch and brief summary of Hawking's work.

O'Connor, J. J., and E. F. Robertson. "Stephen William Hawking." MacTutor History of Mathematics Archive, University of Saint Andrews. Available online. URL: http://www-groups. dcs.st-andrews.ac.uk/~history/Mathematicians/Hawking.html. Accessed January 27, 2003. Biography provided by the University of Saint Andrews, Scotland.

White, Michael, and John Gribbin. *Stephen Hawking: A Life in Science*. New York: Penguin, 1992. Biography of Hawking and a thorough discussion of his early work.

Shing-Tung Yau

6

(1949–)

Shing-Tung Yau solved many open problems in differential geometry and introduced a class of mathematical surfaces known as Calabi-Yau manifolds. (*Kris Snibbe/Harvard News Office*)

Surfaces in Differential Geometry

Shing-Tung Yau (pronounced YOW) developed new ideas and methods in differential geometry and used them to solve many open problems. He proved the Calabi conjecture and introduced Calabi-Yau manifolds as important concepts in mathematical physics. His proof of the positive mass conjecture helped establish a firm mathematical basis for the theory of black holes. In collaboration with other colleagues, he solved Plateau's problem, the Frankel conjecture, and Hitchin-Kobayashi conjecture in differential geometry. He also made discoveries about minimal surfaces, eigenvalues of manifolds, and mirror symmetries. His work in geometry impacted research in many areas of mathematics and physics, including topology, algebraic geometry, general relativity, astronomy, and string theory.

Student of Mathematics

Shing-Tung Yau was born on April 4, 1949, in Shantou, a city in Guangdong Province, southern China. When he was an infant his family moved to Hong Kong, where his father, Chen Ying Chiou, became a professor of economics and philosophy at the Chinese University of Hong Kong (CUHK). Yeuk-Lam Leung Chiou, his mother, sold hand-crafted goods to supplement her husband's low salary and to help support their eight children. At the local high school that Yau attended, the science laboratories were poorly equipped. Consequently, the science curriculum emphasized mathematics, a subject his father encouraged him to study.

In 1966 Yau enrolled as a mathematics major at Chung Chi College, a small undergraduate institution in Hong Kong. Because the college offered a limited number of mathematics courses, he also audited classes at United College and at CUHK. In 1969 he earned his bachelor's degree in mathematics and entered the graduate school at the University of California at Berkeley on a fellowship from International Business Machines (IBM). He earned his Ph.D. in mathematics in 1971, completing a dissertation titled "On the Fundamental Group of Compact Manifolds of Nonpositive Curvature" under the direction of Chinese mathematician Shiing-Shen Chern. Published in the *Annals of Mathematics* in 1971, his doctoral research analyzed algebraic structures associated with manifolds, which are general types of geometrical surfaces.

Solutions to Open Problems in Differential Geometry

During the first 16 years of his professional career, Yau was affiliated with four different academic institutions. He conducted research as a postdoctoral fellow for the 1971–72 academic year at the Institute for Advanced Study (IAS) in Princeton, New Jersey. After a two-year appointment as an assistant professor at the State University of New York at Stony Brook, he spent five years at Stanford University in California, where he quickly earned a promotion from associate professor to professor. He returned to the IAS in 1979 for a five-year period as a professor of mathematics. From 1984 to 1987 he was Chancellor Associate Chair and Professor of Mathematics at the University of California at San Diego (UCSD). During this period he received two prestigious research awards: an Alfred P. Sloan Fellowship for the 1975–76 academic year and a 1980 John Simon Guggenheim Fellowship. In 1976 he married Yu Yun Kuo, whom he had met when they were students at Berkeley. Yau and his wife have two children.

Between 1978 and 1982 Yau established his reputation as a research mathematician by solving three open problems in differential geometry, the branch of mathematics that uses derivatives and integrals to describe and analyze geometrical objects in higher-dimensional spaces. In his 1978 paper "On the Ricci Curvature of a Compact Kähler Manifold and the Complex Monge-Ampère Equation," published in the journal *Communications on Pure and Applied Mathematics*, he solved the Calabi conjecture. The question, first suggested in the 1950s by Italian mathematician Eugenio Calabi, concerned how volume and distance could be measured for certain types of surfaces in five or more dimensions. Yau proved that under the conditions that Calabi had suggested, surfaces known as compact Kähler manifolds had a special type of distance function known as a Ricci-flat metric. To prove this fact, Yau showed that the nonlinear differential equation known as the complex Monge-Ampère equation had a solution for these surfaces. His colleagues in the field of differential geometry praised his achievement as a powerful and significant result. This class of surfaces, now called Calabi-Yau manifolds, are widely studied by mathematical physicists in connection with string theory, the concept that strings of matter form the fundamental building blocks of all substances.

After resolving the Calabi conjecture, Yau collaborated with his former student Richard Schoen to prove the positive mass conjecture. This proposal from Riemannian geometry and Albert

Einstein's general theory of relativity asserts that the sum of all the energy in the universe is positive. In their joint paper "On the Proof of the Positive Mass Conjecture in General Relativity," published in 1979 in the journal *Communications in Mathematical Physics,* they proved a special case of the conjecture for hypersurfaces having zero mean curvature, a restricted class of surfaces whose tangent lines satisfy basic numerical conditions. Their paper "Proof of the Positive Mass Theorem II," which appeared in the same journal in 1981, proved the general case of the conjecture by deforming more general surfaces into the special case that they had resolved earlier. Their proof used new techniques that Yau had developed to analyze the behavior of minimal surfaces in space-time, surfaces with minimum area that satisfy a specified set of conditions. These techniques led to new methods for working with complicated equations known as nonlinear elliptic partial differential equations in geometry, mathematical physics, and topology. Yau and Schoen applied their results to the theory of black holes in their 1983 paper "The Existence of a Black Hole Due to the Condensation of Matter," which appeared in *Communications in Mathematical Physics.* In this paper they proved that when a sufficient amount of matter is condensed in a small region, the resulting gravitational effects will be strong enough to cause the collection of matter to collapse and form a black hole.

In the early 1980s Yau and American mathematician William A. Meeks collaborated on the solution of an open question involving minimal surfaces and Plateau's problem. Named after Joseph Plateau, a 19th-century Belgian physicist who experimented with soap films on wire frames, the question asks for the construction of a surface with minimum area that fits a given boundary. After many mathematicians had studied the problem, research done in the 1930s and 1940s by the American Jesse Douglas, the Hungarian Tibor Radó, and Charles Morrey, also American, had resolved the question of when a solution existed. Yau and Meeks finalized the remaining unanswered questions about these solutions in their paper "The Classical Plateau Problem and the Topology of Three-Dimensional Manifolds. The Embedding of the Solution Given by Douglas-Morrey and an Analytic Proof of Dehn's Lemma," published in 1982 in the journal *Topology.* In this paper they proved

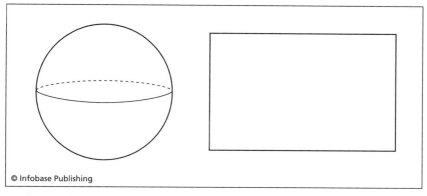

A sphere and a rectangle are examples of minimal surfaces. Any other surface that encloses the same volume as a given sphere must have a larger surface area. When a rectangular wire frame is dipped into a solution of soap and water, the soap will form a flat film that is the surface of minimum area having the frame as its boundary.

that the entire surface produced by Douglas's solution was a smooth surface in ordinary three-dimensional space, a result that Douglas had been able to prove only for localized sections of his surface. In their later papers on the subject, Yau and Meeks extended their analysis to other curves and surfaces in higher dimensions known as loops and spheres.

Yau's work on partial differential equations, the topology of differentiable manifolds, and the properties of minimal surfaces earned him recognition from a number of professional societies. In 1981 the American Mathematical Society (AMS) awarded him its Oswald Veblen Prize in Geometry, and the National Academy of Sciences (NAS) presented him the John J. Carty Award for the Advancement of Science. The International Mathematical Union awarded him the 1982 Fields Medal, the most prestigious honor in mathematics. Comparable in stature to the Nobel Prize, the Fields Medal is awarded to a mathematician under the age of 40 in recognition of past achievement and future promise. In 1983 the American Academy of Arts and Sciences (AAAS) elected him a fellow, and in 1984 *Science Digest* named him one of the 100 brightest scientists under the age of 40. He won a 1985 John D. and Catherine T. MacArthur Fellowship, an award that provided him an annual research stipend of $60,000 for each of the next five years.

In 1986 the AMS invited him to present the Colloquium Lectures at its 90th Summer Meeting.

Analyzing Properties of Manifolds

In addition to the high-profile problems whose solutions earned him widespread recognition and prestigious awards, Yau made significant discoveries in other areas of differential geometry. With Shiu-Yuen Cheng, a mathematician from Hong Kong, he investigated properties of the curvature of complex manifolds in high-dimensional spaces. Their 1976 paper titled "On the Regularity of the Solution of the n-Dimensional Minkowski Problem," which was published in *Communications on Pure and Applied Mathematics*, resolved the question originally posed by 19th-century Russian mathematician Hermann Minkowski of whether a function defined on the surface of an n-dimensional sphere can be extended to all points in the interior of the sphere in more than one way. Canadian mathematician Louis Nirenberg, who had solved the two-dimensional version of this problem, praised Yau and Cheng for the technical power of their methods and for the useful estimates their work produced.

In collaboration with Harvard University mathematician Yum-Tong Siu, Yau coauthored a series of six research papers between 1976 and 1982 on a question about the curvature of manifolds. In their paper "Compact Kähler Manifolds of Positive Bisectional Curvature," which appeared in 1980 in the journal *Inventiones Mathematicae* (Mathematical inventions), they used results from the theory of minimal surfaces to prove the Frankel conjecture. This proposition asserted that the only compact Kähler manifold having a particular curvature property was the well-known complex projective space. Using harmonic maps—functions whose partial derivatives satisfy certain properties—they successfully proved that the conjecture was true. In their other joint papers they investigated manifolds with different curvature properties.

Yau and mathematician Peter Li, who had also been a student at Chern's at Berkeley, conducted collaborative research on numerical characteristics of surfaces known as eigenvalues. In a paper titled "Estimates of Eigenvalues of a Compact Riemannian Manifold" that they presented at the 1979 AMS-sponsored Symposium on Pure Mathematics in Hawaii, they derived precise estimates for the eigenvalues of classes of manifolds based on a small amount of geometrical information about the curvature of the surfaces. In the paper "On the Upper Estimate of the Heat Kernel of a Complete Riemannian Manifold," published in 1981 in the *American Journal of Mathematics*, Yau, Li, and Cheng investigated the heat kernel, another numerical characteristic related to the curvature of a surface.

With American mathematician Karen Uhlenbeck, Yau used ideas from particle physics to analyze four-dimensional manifolds. In their 1986 paper "On the Existence of Hermitian Yang-Mills Connections in Stable Bundles," which was published in *Communications on Pure and Applied Mathematics*, they established a connection between higher-dimensional manifolds satisfying certain topological conditions and functions providing metrics for the surfaces. In the 1950s Chinese physicist Chen Ning Yang and American physicist Robert Mills had introduced the Yang-Mills equation that explained the behavior of elementary particles. The joint paper of Uhlenbeck and Yau proved the Hitchin-Kobayashi conjecture by showing that for compact Kähler manifolds, there is a one-to-one correspondence between stable vector bundles—collections of functions defined on the manifold—and distance functions that satisfy the Yang-Mills equation.

Recent Work in Geometry

In 1987 Yau left UCSD to accept a position at Harvard University in Cambridge, Massachusetts. After holding an endowed chair at Harvard as the Higgins Professor of Mathematics from 1997 to 2000, he assumed his present position in 2000 as the William Casper Graustein Professor of Mathematics. As a John Harvard Fellow in 1996, he spent a year at the Isaac Newton Institute for Mathematical Science at Cambridge University, in England. In 1999 he was the Samuel Eilenberg Visiting Professor at Columbia University, and in 2000 he visited the California Institute of Technology as the Gordon Moore Visiting Professor.

In addition to fulfilling the duties associated with his faculty positions in the United States, Yau worked to improve the level of mathematical education and research in China. He spent the academic year 1991–92 as a visiting professor at CUHK and as chair of the mathematics department at National Tsing Hua University in Taiwan. In collaboration with leaders of the Chinese mathematical community, he helped establish the Institute of Mathematical Sciences (IMS) at CUHK in 1993 and has served as its director since 1994. To honor two of his undergraduate professors, he established the H. L. Chow Mathematics Scholarship and the S. Salaff Mathematics Scholarship at CUHK. He also created the Shiing-Shen Chern Educational Fund at the IMS in memory of his dissertation adviser and endowed two educational funds in remembrance of his parents. Since 2003 he has held the position of Distinguished Professor-at-Large at CUHK.

At the 1991 Symposium on the Current State and Prospects of Mathematics, Yau and six other winners of the Fields Medal were asked to share their assessments of the present and future status of various branches of mathematics. In his address, "The Current State and Prospects of Geometry and Nonlinear Differential Equations," published with the other winners' thoughts in 1992 in the collection *Mathematical Research Today and Tomorrow: Viewpoints of Seven Fields Medalists*, he observed that these fields are active areas of important research. In particular, he cited their increasing use as fundamental tools in computer graphics, particle physics, robotics, chemistry, information theory, weather prediction, and biological modeling.

In 1992 Yau edited the volume *Chern: A Great Geometer of the Twentieth Century*, a collection of papers written by dozens of mathematicians and dedicated to Chern on the occasion of his 79th birthday. The final item in the compilation was Yau's paper "Open Problems in Geometry," an updated version of a previous list of 120 problems in differential geometry that he had identified and publicized 13 years earlier. In 2000 he published a further revision of this list, also titled "Open Problems in Geometry," in the *Journal of the Ramanujan Mathematical Society*. These lists have provided direction and inspiration to researchers in the field of geometry for more than 25 years.

Another of Yau's continuing initiatives has been to compile and circulate the most recent research on mirror symmetry, an area of algebraic geometry and mathematical physics that is related to his work on minimal surfaces. Between 1992 and 2002 he coedited four collections of research papers in this area under the titles *Mirror Symmetry I, II, III, IV.* He has also been an active contributor to this research area, coauthoring with mathematicians Bong Lian of Brandeis University and Kefeng Liu of Stanford University a series of four papers titled "Mirror Principle I, II, III, IV" that appeared between 1997 and 2000 in *The Asian Journal of Mathematics.* In their joint work they investigated the properties of three-dimensional Calabi-Yau manifolds by analyzing the corresponding properties of their more accessible "mirror manifolds."

Yau's research accomplishments have earned him numerous awards and prizes over the past 15 years. Germany's Alexander von Humboldt Foundation awarded him the 1991 Humboldt Research Award. In 1993 the NAS inducted him as a member and the AAAS elected him as a fellow. The Royal Swedish Academy of Sciences awarded him its 1994 Crafoord Prize, citing his development of nonlinear techniques in differential geometry that led to the solution of several outstanding problems. In 1997 U.S. president Bill Clinton presented Yau with the National Science Foundation's National Medal of Science, an award based on the total impact of an individual's work in an area of science or mathematics. He recently received the 2003 International Scientific and Technological Cooperation Award. The Chinese Academy of Sciences, the Russian Academy of Sciences, and the National Academy of Lincei, Italy, have elected him as a foreign member of their academies. Nine universities have awarded him honorary degrees, and eight universities in China have made him an honorary professor.

During his 35-year career Yau has written more than 300 papers and has edited volumes of papers. He has directed the doctoral dissertations of more than 30 graduate students at Harvard, UCSD, Princeton, CUHK, Stanford, the Massachusetts Institute of Technology, and Brandeis University. He has helped guide the direction of research in his field by serving as editor in chief of both the *Journal of Differential Geometry* and the *Asian Journal of Mathematics* and as an editor for the journals *Communications in Mathematical Physics, Letters in Mathematical Physics,* and *Communications in Information and Systems.*

Conclusion

Shing-Tung Yau has made substantial contributions to the field of differential geometry. The techniques he has developed have changed the way partial differential equations are used as a tool in the analysis of geometrical problems. His proof of the Calabi conjecture established Calabi-Yau manifolds as an important research topic in mathematical physics. He helped to solidify the mathematical basis of the theory of black holes by his proof of the positive mass conjecture. His resolution of Plateau's problem, the Frankel conjecture, and the Hitchin-Kobayashi conjecture provided solutions to long-standing open problems. Yau's work in geometry has impacted research in diverse branches of mathematics and physics, including topology, algebraic geometry, the theory of minimal surfaces, general relativity, astronomy, and string theory.

FURTHER READING

Nicholson, F. C., and Loretta Hall. "Shing-Tung Yau, 1949– , Chinese-born American Differential Geometer." In *Notable Mathematicians: From Ancient Times to the Present*, edited by Robyn V. Young, 519–521. Detroit, Mich.: Gale, 1998. Brief but informative profile of Yau and his most important work.

Nirenberg, Louis. "The Work of Shing-Tung Yau." *Notices of the American Mathematical Society* 29 (1982): 501–502. Brief summary of six of Yau's achievements.

O'Connor, J. J., and E. F. Robertson. "Shing-Tung Yau." MacTutor History of Mathematics Archive, University of Saint Andrews. Available online. URL: http://www-groups.dcs.st-andrews.ac.uk/~history/Mathematicians/Yau.html. Accessed March 14, 2003. Biography provided by the University of Saint Andrews, Scotland.

"Shing-Tung Yau." Wikipedia, the Free Encyclopedia. Available online. URL: http://en.wikipedia.org/wiki/S._T._Yau. Accessed October 28, 2005. Brief biography with links to other Web sites and additional explanations.

Stern, R., and G. Tian. "Donaldson and Yau Receive Crafoord Prize." *Notices of the American Mathematical Society* 41 (1994): 794–796. Summary of Yau's research accomplishments.

7

Fan Chung

(1949–)

Fan Chung patented a technique for encoding and decoding cellular telephone calls and analyzed the mathematical properties involved in Internet computing. *(Courtesy of Fan Chung)*

Professor of Internet Mathematics

Fan Chung made contributions to the mathematical analysis of graphs and telecommunications networks as a mathematician in both industrial and academic settings. Her discoveries in Ramsey theory revealed new information about coloring the edges of graphs. She obtained a patent for encoding and decoding techniques that enable cellular telephone calls to be transmitted efficiently and securely. She analyzed the efficiency of Steiner trees and of algorithms to manipulate graphs and networks. Her research in spectral theory and random graphs has provided a deeper understanding of the mathematical properties of Internet computing.

Student of Mathematics

Fan Rong King was born on October 9, 1949, in Kaoshiung, Taiwan, to Yuan Shang King, a mechanical engineer, and Wu Chi King, a high school home economics teacher. Her father encouraged her and her younger brother, Tom, to pursue careers involving practical applications of mathematics. Observing her mother's dedication to her students and her profession, she also developed an interest in becoming a teacher. After attending the local elementary and middle schools, she enrolled at Kaoshiung Girls' High School, where she excelled in geometry and physics and placed as the top student on standardized aptitude tests.

King's academic performance in high school earned her admission to the highly selective mathematics program at National Taiwan University. After a year of general studies, the institution's intensive curriculum focused exclusively on mathematics. During these years she acquired an interest in combinatorics, the branch of mathematics concerned with sophisticated counting techniques that enable mathematicians to understand the numerical characteristics of discrete structures. Solving problems and studying with her fellow students, she developed skills for effective collaboration and communication of technical material. After earning her bachelor of science degree in mathematics in 1970, she traveled to the United States to pursue graduate studies.

At the University of Pennsylvania in Philadelphia, King continued to excel as a graduate student, earning her master's degree in mathematics in 1972. During the following year she married and became known as Fan Chung. On the qualifying examinations that permit students to continue studying for their doctoral degree, she obtained the highest score among all graduate students in the mathematics department. Professor Herbert Wilf introduced her to some ideas in Ramsey theory, the area of combinatorics concerned with how large a collection of objects must be in order to guarantee that it satisfies particular conditions. Within a week she produced a proof that generalized a major theorem and became the central portion of her dissertation. She explained her results in a presentation titled "On Triangular and Cyclic Ramsey Numbers with k Colors" that she delivered in 1973 at the Capital Conference at George Washington University in Washington, D.C., and in the paper "On the Ramsey Numbers $N(3, 3, \ldots 3; 2)$" that appeared later that year in the journal *Discrete Mathematics.*

The problem concerned complete graphs on n vertices, collections of n points or vertices that are connected to one another by line segments called edges. Chung's theorem addressed the question: If each edge is assigned one of k colors, how many vertices must the graph have to guarantee that there are three vertices joined by three edges of a single color? She showed that a four-coloring of a complete graph must have more than 50 vertices in order to guarantee the existence of a single-colored triangle. Chung proved additional results that related the minimum sizes of such graphs when they are colored with k, $k - 2$, and $k + 1$ colors. She incorporated these discoveries and further research on related problems in her 1974 doctoral dissertation, "Ramsey Numbers and Combinatorial Designs," that earned her a Ph.D. in mathematics.

Industrial Mathematician

Chung spent the next 16 years conducting research as a mathematician in the telecommunications field. From 1974 to 1983 she worked as a member of the technical staff in the Mathematical Foundations of Computing Department at Bell Laboratories in Murray Hill, New Jersey. In 1984 she joined Bell Communications Research (Bellcore) in Morristown, New Jersey, as manager of the Discrete Mathematics Research Group. From 1986 to 1990 she served as division manager for Mathematics, Information Sciences, and Operations Research at Bellcore. In these positions she conducted research individually and in collaboration with other colleagues in the areas of Ramsey theory, graph theory, and combinatorics with emphasis on applications to telecommunications networks, electronic circuits, and computer algorithms. As a manager, she recruited other mathematicians and supervised their research.

Continuing her investigations in Ramsey theory, Chung and her Bell Labs colleague Ronald Graham coauthored the paper "On

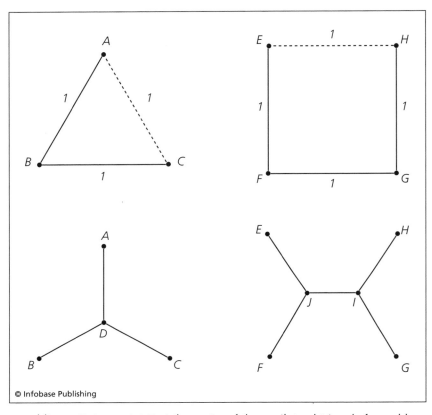

© Infobase Publishing

By adding a Steiner point *D* at the center of the equilateral triangle formed by the three points *A*, *B*, and *C*, the four vertices can be connected by a Steiner tree of total length $\sqrt{3} \approx 1.7$ that is more efficient than the spanning tree of length 2. Adding two Steiner points *I* and *J* to a square arrangement of four points *E*, *F*, *G*, and *H* results in a Steiner tree of total length $1 + \sqrt{3} \approx 2.7$ rather than a spanning tree of total length 3.

Multicolor Ramsey Numbers for Complete Bipartite Graphs," which was published in 1975 in the *Journal of Combinatorial Theory*. Their joint work presented properties of Ramsey numbers for bipartite graphs, graphs in which the vertices are partitioned into two sets so that every edge joins a node from one set with a node from the other. This paper was the first of more than 60 research papers jointly written by the two mathematicians, who married in 1983.

In the area of graph theory Chung obtained new results about the efficiency of networks built from minimal spanning trees and minimal Steiner trees. For a graph representing n telephone customers connected by a system of phone lines, n computers connected by a network of cables, or n electronic components wired together on an integrated circuit chip, a minimal spanning tree is a set of $n - 1$ edges connecting all the vertices while having the smallest total length. A minimum Steiner tree improves on this optimal subset of edges by introducing new vertices and edges that result in a smaller total edge length. At the 1976 Conference on Algorithmic Aspects of Combinatorics, Chung and Graham presented a joint paper titled "Steiner Trees for Ladders" in which they explained how to construct minimum Steiner trees if the vertices lie in corresponding pairs on two parallel lines. In the 1978 paper "A Lower Bound for the Steiner Tree Problem," published in the *Society for Industrial and Applied Mathematics (SIAM) Journal on Applied Mathematics*, she and Bellcore research colleague Frank Hwang proved that the minimum Steiner tree of a graph cannot produce a savings of more than 26 percent compared to the length of the minimal spanning tree. She and Graham improved this bound in their 1985 paper "A New Bound for Euclidean Steiner Minimal Trees," which appeared in the *Annals of the New York Academy of Sciences*, by proving that Steiner trees cannot generate a savings of more than 18 percent. In the 1989 article "Steiner Trees on a Checkerboard," published in *Mathematics Magazine*, Chung, Graham, and American mathematician Martin Gardner described the minimum Steiner tree for a graph laid out like the squares of an $n \times n$ checkerboard. The Mathematical Association of America (MAA) honored the three authors by awarding them the 1990 Carl B. Allendoerfer Award for expository writing.

Telecommunications Networks and Algorithms

Chung used the techniques of graph theory and combinatorics to investigate and solve a range of problems presented by telecommunications networks. In the 1977 paper "On Blocking Probabilities for Switching Networks," published in the *Bell System Technical Journal*, she and Hwang presented several techniques for determining the likelihood that an intermediate network of switches does not provide an open path connecting a specified pair of nodes. At the American Mathematical Society's (AMS) 1984 Conference on the Mathematics of Information Processing, she presented a paper titled "Diameters of Communications Networks" that discussed algorithms for reducing the number of links over which a message travels in a network. With Sandeep Bhatt, a Bellcore colleague, and Arny Rosenberg, an American computer scientist, she cowrote the paper "Partitioning Circuits for Improved Testability" that appeared in *Advanced Research in VLSI*, a volume of papers about a design technique for integrated circuits known as very large scale integration. Their article discussed methods for uniformly distributing the processing work among the registers of a computer circuit. In 1987 she, Rosenberg, and Frank Leighton, an American applied mathematician, coauthored the paper "Embedding Graphs in Books: A Layout Problem with Applications to VLSI Design," which appeared in the *SIAM Journal of Algebraic Discrete Methods*. This paper presented their collaborative research on conditions that allow the edges of a graph to be arranged like the pages of a book and discussed the implications for incorporating such graphs into chip designs.

Chung investigated algorithms for solving other types of problems that arise in discrete mathematics. With the Americans Michael Garey, a mathematician, and David Johnson, a computer scientist, she coauthored the paper "On Packing Two-Dimensional Bins" that was published in 1982 in the *SIAM Journal on Algorithms and Discrete Methods*. Their paper presented a new method for efficiently arranging rectangular objects of assorted sizes into a minimum number of larger rectangles without any overlapping areas. In 1985 she collaborated with Bellcore researcher Dan Hajela and British mathematician Paul Seymour on the article "Self-Organizing Sequential Search and Hilbert's Inequalities" for the Association of Computing Machinery's (ACM) Seventeenth Annual Symposium on the Theory of Computing. Their joint research analyzed the work involved in accessing information stored in a linear list. For the 1986 conference Discrete Algorithms and Complexity in Kyoto, Japan, she coauthored the paper "Dynamic Search in Graphs" with Graham and Michael Saks, a mathematician from Rutgers University. In this paper they discussed the difficulty of finding data in a graph whose structure changes in response to its history of requests.

During her years at Bell Labs and Bellcore, Chung developed commercially viable innovations that earned her two patents. In 1988 she was granted a patent for developing a system for encoding and decoding audio messages so they can be reliably transmitted through a communications network using the technique of code division multiple access (CDMA). Her encoding and decoding scheme allowed multiple cellular phone conversations to securely share a common radio frequency by matching each call with a different cellular antenna. In addition to data security, another important aspect of her encoding-decoding process was that it could be rapidly implemented to maintain the natural sound of the caller's voice. In 1993 she received a second patent for developing a method for routing network traffic.

Academic Researcher

After working in the telecommunications industry for 15 years, Chung changed the direction of her career to become a university professor. In 1989 she taught computer science courses as a visiting professor at Princeton University in Princeton, New Jersey. From 1990 to 1994 she was a Bellcore Fellow at Harvard University in Cambridge, Massachusetts, where she studied for a year and taught mathematics courses as a visiting professor for two years. In 1994 she left Bellcore and spent a year conducting research at the Institute for Advanced Study in Princeton. From 1995 to 1998 Chung held an endowed chair as both a professor of mathematics and a professor of computer science at the University of Pennsylvania. In 1998 she moved to the University of California at San Diego (UCSD), where she currently holds a position as professor of mathematics, professor of computer science and engineering, and Akamai Professor in Internet mathematics. At UCSD she has developed new courses to bridge the gap between the theoretical mathematics that is often taught at universities and the mathematics that is needed for commercial applications.

In both her research and her teaching Chung emphasized connections between mathematics and the disciplines of science and engineering. Her article "Should You Prepare Differently for a Nonacademic Career?" which was published in 1991 in the *Notices of the American Mathematical Society*, counseled students studying mathematics who were not intending to pursue careers in education to obtain a broad knowledge of mathematics that can be utilized in diverse applied contexts. In the paper "Mathematics and the Buckyball" that appeared in 1993 in the *American Scientist*, she and Harvard University mathematician Shlomo Sternberg analyzed the mathematical properties of the carbon-60 molecule whose geometrical shape is known as a buckyball. Their article included a diagram of 20 hexagons linked with 12 pentagons that readers could cut out and assemble into a soccer ball–shaped polyhedron.

During the 1990s Chung published three books about general topics in graph theory and combinatorics. In 1991, with Graham and mathematicians Yousef Alavi and D. Frank Hsu, she coauthored the book *Graph Theory, Combinatorics, Algorithms, and Applications* that presented a summary of recent work in these related areas of mathematics. With mathematicians Béla Bollobás of Cambridge University and Persi Diaconis of Stanford University she coedited the 1992 conference proceedings *Probabilistic Combinatorics and Its Applications*. This work compiled a collection of seven papers that presented classical results and recent developments on random graphs, graphs in which the existence of an edge between any two vertices is randomly determined by a probability distribution. In 1998 she and Graham wrote the book *Erdös on Graphs, His Legacy of Unsolved Problems* in which they collected all the open problems in graph theory that Hungarian mathematician Paul Erdös had posed and promised to pay the prize money that he had offered for each problem's solution. Chung had already coauthored 12 papers with Erdös, who was a frequent house guest when he was not traveling to attend international conferences or to collaborate with his extensive network of research partners.

Chung published a steady stream of papers detailing her continued research on graph theory and networks. With Graham and Bellcore colleague Noga Alon she coauthored the paper "Routing Permutations on Graphs via Matchings" that appeared in 1994 in the *SIAM Journal on Discrete Mathematics*. This paper analyzed the problem of sending information from each vertex in a graph to a different vertex using nonoverlapping sets of edges at each stage of the multiple step process. In 1997 she and Bhatt wrote a paper titled "On Optimal Strategies for Cycle-Stealing in Networks of Workstations," which was published in the *Institute of Electrical and Electronics Engineers (IEEE) Transactions on Computers.* In this paper they analyzed the increased productivity generated by allowing computers operating in a parallel configuration to borrow processing time from one another. Chung teamed with Bhatt, Rosenberg, and AT&T researchers William Aiello and Ramesh Sitaraman to write the paper "Augmented Ring Networks," appearing in 2001 in the *IEEE Transactions on Parallel and Distributed Systems.* This paper examined multiple methods for improving the performance of a collection of computers that were sequentially linked to each other.

Spectral Graph Theory and Internet Mathematics

Chung expanded her research interests to spectral graph theory, the branch of graph theory concerned with the development and application of numerical measures that characterize the properties of graphs. At the 1991 AMS-MAA joint summer meetings, she presented a lecture titled "Laplacians of Graphs and Hypergraphs" that the AMS recorded and distributed as part of its video lecture series. In her presentation she described how to use the information in the Laplacian matrix about the degree of interconnectedness between the vertices of a graph and the vertices of a more general structure known as a hypergraph. Her 1997 book *Spectral Graph Theory* presented a unified treatment of this area of mathematics, emphasizing conclusions that can be drawn from an analysis of the numerical quantities known as the eigenvalues of a graph's Laplacian. In the paper "Spanning Trees in Subgraphs of Lattices" that she presented at the 1997 AMS conference Applications of Curves over Finite Fields, she used Laplacians to estimate the number of spanning trees for subsets of graphs known as lattices. With French mathematicians Charles Delorme and Patrick Solé she wrote the paper "Multidiameters and Multiplicities," which was published in the *European Journal of Combinatorics.* This paper analyzed the construction of large graphs with a specified diameter, the length of the shortest sequence of edges joining any two vertices.

As Akamai Professor in Internet mathematics at UCSD, Chung's recent research has focused on the mathematical analysis of the international network of computers that form the World Wide Web. In the paper "Dynamic Location Problems with Limited Look-Ahead" that she and Graham presented at the 1998 Computing and Combinatorics Conference in Taipei, Taiwan, she examined the efficiency of a network of computers that do not satisfy requests for service until they examine the past history of requests and preview a portion of the list of pending requests. This problem arises in connection with the management of visits to Web pages. Chung and Graham collaborated with Mark Garrett and David Shallcross, two electrical engineers at Telcordia Technologies in New Jersey to research and write the paper "Distance Realization Problems with Applications to Internet Tomography," which appeared in 2001 in the *Journal of Computer and System Sciences.* This paper presented their research on graphs in which vertices are linked by sequences of edges of specified lengths and some related issues that arise in the analysis of Internet data traffic models. In 2003 Chung collaborated with her UCSD colleagues Linyuan Lu and Van Vu on the article "Eigenvalues of Random Power Law Graphs," published in the *Annals of Combinatorics.* They analyzed the numerical characteristics of randomly generated graphs in which the number of vertices having k edges is proportional to some power of k. These graphs occur in the patterns of e-mail traffic as well as in biological networks. With Graham and Lu she coauthored the paper "Guessing Secrets with Inner Product Questions" that appeared in 2004 in the journal *Internet Mathematics.* This paper analyzed algorithms by which a seeker can obtain information from an adversary who tries to reveal as little information as possible.

In addition to her teaching and research, Chung has served the mathematical community as an editor of journals and as a member of numerous committees and boards for many professional societies. As coeditor in chief of the journals *Advances in Applied Mathematics, Internet Mathematics,* and the *Electronic Journal of Combinatorics* and as a member of the editorial boards of 11 other academic journals, she reviews the work of many researchers and helps determine the direction of future research. From 1990 to 1993 she served on the executive committee of the National Science Foundation's Center on Discrete Mathematics and Theoretical Computer Science (DIMACS). In the early 1990s she served on the organizing committees for the Symposium on Discrete Algorithms and the Symposium on the Theory of Computing. Throughout the 1990s Chung held a variety of leadership positions in professional societies, including chairing the AMS Conference Board on Mathematical Sciences, the MAA's Putnam Questions Committee, and the SIAM Activity Group in Discrete Mathematics. She continues to serve on the board of governors of the Institute of Mathematics and Its Applications and on the advisory board of the New York Academy of Sciences.

In her career Chung has written four books and more than 200 research papers. Her collaborators include mathematicians, computer scientists, statisticians, and chemists. She mentored many researchers during her years at Bellcore and has supervised the doctoral dissertations of four graduate students during the academic portion of her career. In 1998 the American Academy of Arts and Sciences elected her as a fellow.

Conclusion

During her years as a mathematician in both industry and academia, Fan Chung has contributed new research results to the areas of combinatorics, graph theory, networks, and Internet mathematics. In analyzing Ramsey numbers she made new discoveries about graph coloring. Her encoding and decoding techniques for CDMA provided a method for efficiently and securely transmitting cell phone calls. She analyzed the efficiency of Steiner trees and of algorithms to manipulate graphs and networks. Her continued work in spectral theory and random graphs provides a deeper understanding of the mathematical properties of the Internet and the World Wide Web.

FURTHER READING

Albers, Donald. "Making Connections. A Profile of Fan Chung." *Math Horizons*, September 1995, pp. 14–18. Brief profile of

Chung, with insight into her work and her approach to mathematical research.

Bates, Karl Leif. "Fan R. K. Chung, 1949– , Taiwan-born American Number Theorist." In *Notable Mathematicians: From Ancient Times to the Present,* edited by Robyn V. Young, 115–117. Detroit, Mich.: Gale, 1998. Brief profile of Chung and discussion of some of her industrial work.

Brunner, Regina Baron. "Fan King Chung." In *Notable Women in Mathematics: A Biographical Dictionary,* edited by Charlene Morrow and Teri Perl, 29–34. Westport, Conn.: Greenwood Press, 1998. Short biography of Chung.

Henrion, Claudia. "Fan Chung (1949–)." In *Women in Mathematics: The Addition of Difference,* 96–107. Bloomington: Indiana University Press, 1997. Biographical profile offering insight into her career as a mathematician.

O'Connor, J. J., and E. F. Robertson. "Fan Rong K Chung Graham." MacTutor History of Mathematics Archive, University of Saint Andrews. Available online. URL: http://www-groups. dcs.st-andrews.ac.uk/~history/Mathematicians/Chung.html. Accessed March 14, 2003. Biography provided by the University of Saint Andrews, Scotland.

8

Andrew Wiles

(1953–   )

Andrew Wiles used modular forms and elliptic curves to prove Fermat's last theorem. *(Denise Applewhite/ CORBIS SYGMA)*

Number Theorist Who Proved Fermat's Last Theorem

After working in isolation for seven years, Andrew Wiles proved Fermat's last theorem by solving a related conjecture about modular elliptic curves. His resolution of this problem from number theory that had remained unsolved for more than 300 years brought him international fame. Before this celebrated achievement, he had made significant contributions to algebraic number theory through his work on Iwasawa theory and the Birch and Swinnerton-Dyer conjecture.

Early Interest in Mathematics

Andrew John Wiles was born on April 11, 1953, in Cambridge, England, to Patricia Mowll and Maurice Frank Wiles. Along with his brother and sister he grew up in an academically rich environment. An ordained minister, his father served as dean of Clare College at Cambridge University, as professor of Christian doctrine at King's College in London, and as Regius Professor of Divinity and a canon of Christ Church at Oxford University.

As a child, Wiles enjoyed solving arithmetic problems at school and creating and solving similar ones at home. At the age of 10 he became fascinated by one particular problem known as Fermat's last theorem, the conjecture that there are no nonzero integers x, y, and z that satisfy the equation $x^n + y^n = z^n$ if n is an integer greater than 2. Inspired by the book *The Last Problem* by Eric Temple Bell that described this famous unsolved problem and its 300-year history, he became determined to solve Fermat's last theorem. During his teenage years he tried to approach the problem using only high school mathematics. As an undergraduate mathematics major at Merton College of Oxford University, he paid particular attention to the mathematical methods that other researchers had used to attack Fermat's last theorem during the three prior centuries. His fascination with this problem led him to deeper studies of mathematics.

Research on Elliptic Curves

After earning his bachelor's degree from Oxford in 1974, Wiles entered the graduate program at Clare College of Cambridge University. In 1975 he passed Part III of the mathematical Tripos, the fourth year of the British comprehensive examinations in mathematics. After earning his master's degree in mathematics in 1977, he spent three years as a junior research fellow at Clare College and a Benjamin Pierce Assistant Professor at Harvard University in Cambridge, Massachusetts. During these years he conducted research under the direction of Cambridge professor John Coates. He chose to specialize in algebraic number theory—the branch of mathematics that employs algebraic technique to investigate prop-

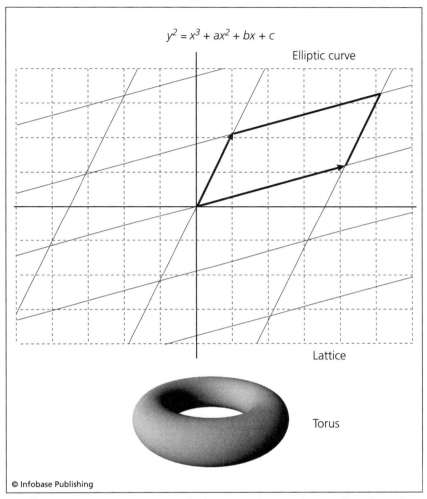

$$y^2 = x^3 + ax^2 + bx + c$$

Elliptic curve

Lattice

Torus

© Infobase Publishing

An elliptic curve generates a periodic lattice in the complex number plane that corresponds to the surface of a bagel-shaped torus.

erties of the integers—with the hope that his work would lead to the solution of Fermat's last theorem.

Coates and Wiles performed joint research on elliptic curves, equations of the form $y^2 = x^3 + ax^2 + bx + c$ where the coefficients a, b, and c are integers. The graph of the points (x, y) that form the solutions of an elliptic curve can be transformed into a two-dimensional region known as a lattice and then formed into a bagel-shaped surface known as a torus. Number theorists analyzing an elliptic curve attempt to determine the number of points with integer coordinates that satisfy its equation and the number of ways to modify algebraically the lattice while preserving the shape of the related torus.

In their early research Coates and Wiles expanded arithmetic results that Austrian mathematician Emil Artin, German mathematician Helmut Hasse, and Japanese mathematician Kenkichi Iwasawa had obtained for one type of algebraic structure and generalized it to a broader class of structures. They described their preliminary findings in the paper "Explicit Reciprocity Laws" that they presented in 1976 at Journées Arithmétiques de Caen (Arithmetic days at Caen), a number theory conference at the University of Caen in France. Wiles provided a more detailed description of their work in his 1978 paper "Higher Explicit Reciprocity Laws," which appeared in the *Annals of Mathematics*. For a pair of integers p and q, a reciprocity law indicates when an expression of the form x^n can be written as both $x^n = p + q \cdot j$ and $x^n = q + p \cdot k$ for some integers j and k. In their papers Coates and Wiles established reciprocity laws when p and q are associated with more complicated algebraic structures.

Wiles and Coates applied their reciprocity results to solve a portion of an outstanding conjecture about elliptic curves. The points on the surface of any elliptic curve can be rearranged by multiplying them by an integer. If a similar rearrangement can also be accomplished by multiplying by a limited collection of complex numbers, mathematicians say that the elliptic curve has complex multiplication. In the 1960s British mathematicians Bryan Birch and Peter Swinnerton-Dyer proposed a conjecture that there is a simple way to determine whether an elliptic curve has a finite or infinite number of rational points, points whose coordinates are fractions or rational numbers. In their paper "On the Conjecture of Birch and Swinnerton-Dyer" that was published in 1977 in the journal *Inventiones Mathematicae* (Mathematical inventions), Coates and Wiles proved half of the weak Birch and Swinnerton-Dyer conjecture for elliptic curves with complex multiplication. Although they did not succeed in proving the entire conjecture, the significance of their work is evident by the fact that in May 2000 the Clay Mathematics Institute announced that this still-unproven conjecture was one of seven "millennium problems" and that the institute would award $1 million for its complete proof.

In 1980 Wiles earned his Ph.D. from Cambridge University for his dissertation, titled "Reciprocity Laws and the Conjecture of Birch and Swinnerton-Dyer," that presented his partial solution of the famous conjecture and his work from his earlier papers on reciprocity laws. His reputation as a rising scholar enabled him to spend the next six years at six different academic institutions in Germany, the United States, and France. In 1981 he was a visiting professor at the Sonderforschungsbereich Theoretische Mathematik (Special research center for theoretical mathematics) in Bonn, Germany. During the 1981–82 academic year he was a member of the Institute for Advanced Study (IAS) in Princeton, New Jersey. After spending the next year as a visiting professor at France's Université de Paris, Orsay (University of Paris at Orsay), he secured an appointment to the mathematics faculty at Princeton University in Princeton, New Jersey. A Guggenheim Fellowship enabled him to travel to Paris for the 1985–86 academic year as a visiting professor at the Institut des Hautes Études Scientifiques (Institute of high scientific studies) and at the École Normale Supérieure (Normal superior university).

Modular Forms and Iwasawa Theory

After completing his dissertation, Wiles realized that he was not making any progress toward the solution of Fermat's last theorem, so he set it aside to concentrate on other topics in algebraic number theory. His research during the next 15 years focused on modular forms and Iwasawa theory. Modular forms are a certain class of elliptic curves that have well-behaved properties related to the curve's lattice. Iwasawa theory is an area of number theory that uses techniques introduced by Iwasawa in the 1950s to establish connections between the structures of collections of numbers and related collections of functions that are known as algebraic number fields and algebraic function fields, respectively.

The most important of Wiles's papers on modular forms and Iwasawa theory was the paper "Class Fields of Abelian Extensions of Q," which he coauthored with American mathematician Barry Mazur. In this 1984 paper published in *Inventiones Mathematicae*, they proved the main conjecture of Iwasawa theory for number fields that were related to the set of all rational numbers. This conjecture asserted that there should be a precise relationship between p-adic zeta functions and Iwasawa modules, two objects associated with any algebraic number field. This paper constituted a major achievement in Iwasawa theory because it produced the first complete proof of the main conjecture for any class of number fields. In 1990 Wiles published a general proof of the main conjecture of Iwasawa theory for fields of real numbers in his paper "The Iwasawa Conjecture for Totally Real Fields," which appeared in the *Annals of Mathematics.*

Wiles's work on the main conjecture of Iwasawa theory and his earlier research results on the Birch and Swinnerton-Dyer conjecture represented major contributions to algebraic number theory. In 1988 the London Mathematical Society awarded him its Whitehead Prize, a recognition reserved for British mathematicians who have achieved significant accomplishments before the age of 40. Wiles returned to England as a Royal Society Research Professor at Oxford from 1988 to 1990. During that time the Royal Society of London elected him as a fellow. He spent the next year at Princeton University and was a visiting researcher at the IAS for the 1991–92 academic year before rejoining the mathematics department at Princeton.

Proof of Fermat's Last Theorem

From 1986 to 1993 Wiles focused his mathematical research exclusively on a single problem: Fermat's last theorem. Although he published a small number of papers during this period, he had in fact completed the research for these papers before 1986 and was publishing his results periodically to disguise the fact that he was devoting all his efforts to one demanding and time-consuming project. When he was not teaching, he worked in isolation in his sparse office in the attic of his home. Only his wife, Nada, whom he married in 1986, and one professional colleague, Princeton mathematics professor Nicholas Katz, knew that he was trying to solve Fermat's last theorem. The problem consumed his thoughts and energies every day. One of his few diversions was playing with his three daughters, Clare, Kate, and Olivia.

Fermat's last theorem—the assertion that there are no integer solutions to the equation $x^n + y^n = z^n$ if the exponent n is an integer greater than two—was one of many statements that 17th-century French number theorist Pierre de Fermat claimed to have proven. Within 150 years after his death mathematicians were able to prove or disprove all his other claims, leaving this as his final unsolved problem. By the middle of the 19th century, researchers in France had proved a special case of Fermat's last theorem for all exponents less than 200 but had been able to prove the full theorem only for $n = 3, 4, 5, 7$, and 14. In 1976 mathematicians showed that Fermat's equation had no integer solutions for all exponents less than 125,000. Sixteen years later, with the help of a computer program, researchers proved that there were no integer solutions for any exponent less than 4,000,000.

The development that inspired Wiles to devote his full attention to Fermat's last theorem was a 1986 paper by American mathematician Kenneth Ribet that linked the problem to an earlier conjecture about elliptic curves. In 1955 Japanese mathematicians Yutaka Taniyama and Goro Shimura had proposed the conjecture that every elliptic curve with rational numbers as coefficients is modular. Ribet connected Fermat's last theorem to elliptic curves by showing that if $a^n + b^n = c^n$ for nonzero integers a, b, and c, then $y^2 = x(x - a^n)(x + b^n)$ formed an elliptic curve that was not modular. This result meant that if the Taniyama-Shimura conjecture was true, then the numbers a, b, and c that satisfied Fermat's equation and produced Ribet's nonmodular elliptic curve could not exist.

In 1993, after seven years of work, Wiles proved a restricted version of the Taniyama-Shimura conjecture. He concentrated on semistable elliptic curves, elliptic curves whose three roots satisfy a particular condition involving prime numbers. Using ideas known as Galois representations, Hecke algebras, discriminants, and j-invariants, he proved that every semistable elliptic curve was modular. Since the elliptic curve $y^2 = x(x - a^n)(x + b^n)$ would be semistable but not modular if $a^n + b^n = c^n$, this result meant that there could not be any such numbers a, b, and c.

Wiles announced the results of his research on June 23, 1993, at a small conference at the Isaac Newton Institute in Cambridge, England. After he presented his proof that every semistable elliptic curve was modular and indicated that this result proved Fermat's last theorem, the audience of 200 mathematicians gave him a standing ovation. The announcement generated excitement throughout the international scientific community until a mathematician discovered a subtle mistake in the proof. During the next 15 months Wiles worked with his former student Richard Taylor to correct the error by replacing that portion of the proof with a valid argument using a different technique. In May 1995 the *Annals of Mathematics* published Wiles's corrected proof in the 109-page paper "Modular Elliptic Curves and Fermat's Last Theorem" and the accompanying 48-page article "Ring-Theoretic Properties of Certain Hecke Algebras" coauthored by Wiles and Taylor.

The significance of Wiles's accomplishment extended beyond his success in proving a theorem that had been an open problem for more than three centuries. His proof provided a partial realization of the Langlands program, an effort initiated in the 1960s by Canadian mathematician Robert Langlands to establish unifying connections between seemingly unrelated branches of mathematics. Encouraged by his success, other mathematicians have begun to apply the techniques of modern algebraic geometry in attempts to solve classical conjectures and open problems from other areas of mathematics.

Wiles's proof of Fermat's last theorem earned him numerous awards and elevated him to the status of a celebrity. In 1993 *People* magazine named him one of the 25 Most Intriguing People of the Year. The following year Princeton appointed him to an endowed chair as the Eugene Higgins Professor of Mathematics and the American Academy of Arts and Sciences elected him as a fellow. He received the 1995 Schock Prize in Mathematics from the Royal Swedish Academy of Sciences, the 1995 Prix Fermat (Fermat prize) from the Université Paul Sabatier (University of Paul Sabatier), the 1996 Wolf Prize, and the 1996 Royal Medal from the Royal Society of London. In 1996 the United States National Academy of Sciences (NAS) inducted him as a foreign member and presented him the NAS Award in Mathematics. The American Mathematical Society (AMS) invited him to present the 1996 Colloquium Lectures at its 100th Summer Meeting and awarded him the 1997 Frank Nelson Cole Prize in Number Theory. The Public Broadcasting System filmed a 1997 documentary titled *The Proof* about his work on Fermat's last theorem. At the 1998 Fields Medal ceremony, the International Mathematical Union presented Wiles a special silver plaque in honor of his achievement. The Clay Mathematics Institute named him the winner of the 1999 Clay Research Award.

Several of the prizes Wiles won provided him substantial financial rewards, in addition to the recognition of his peers. In 1997 he claimed the Wolfskehl Prize, a monetary award that German mathematician Paul Wolfskehl had established in 1908 when he bequeathed 100,000 marks to the University of Göttingen to be awarded for the first complete proof of Fermat's last theorem. The John D. and Catherine T. MacArthur Foundation named him as a fellow for the period 1997 to 2002, a designation that provided him an annual research stipend of $60,000. In 1998 he won the King Faisal International Prize for Science that included an award of $200,000 and a gold medal. The Shaw Prize Foundation of Hong Kong presented him its 2005 Shaw Prize worth $1 million.

Research after Fermat

Wiles continues to teach and conduct research as chair of Princeton's mathematics department. From 1995 to 2004 he also held an appointment as a professor of mathematics at the IAS. Since 1998 he has served on the Scientific Advisory Board of the Clay Mathematics Institute that offers million-dollar prizes for the solutions of seven famous open problems. He has directed the doctoral research of 12 graduate students and has received many invitations to lecture about his work and his perspective on mathematics. Typical of these presentations was his lecture "Twenty Years of Number Theory," a survey of recent work in this branch of mathematics, that he presented in 1998 at the International Congress in Berlin.

In 2001 French mathematician Christophe Breuil and three of Wiles's former doctoral students Brian Conrad, Fred Diamond, and Taylor proved that all elliptic curves are modular, resolving the full Taniyama-Shimura conjecture. Although Wiles did not directly participate in this collaborative research project, their work followed the strategy and used the techniques that he had introduced in his earlier proof of the semistable case.

Wiles has continued to conduct research in algebraic number theory. In a series of papers published between 1997 and 2001, he and Chris Skinner, another of Wiles's former doctoral students, presented their research on properties of modular forms. Their 1997 paper "Ordinary Representations and Modular Forms," published in the *Proceedings of the National Academy of Sciences of the United States of America*, used methods from Wiles's earlier work on Iwasawa theory to prove that certain types of curves are modular. In their paper "Residually Reducible Representations and Modular Forms," which appeared in 2000 in *Institut des Hautes Études Scientifiques. Publications Mathématiques* (Institute of High Scientific Studies, mathematical publications), they presented new techniques to work with modular forms in an attempt to resolve a conjecture proposed by Mazur and the French mathematician Jean-Marc Fontaine. Their two most recent papers—"Base Change and a Problem of Serre," published in 2001 in the *Duke Mathematical Journal*, and "Nearly Ordinary Deformations of Irreducible Residual Representations," which appeared later in the same year in *Toulouse. Faculté des Sciences. Annales Mathématiques* (Toulouse, department of sciences, annals of mathematics)—provided new techniques and additional results involving modular forms.

Conclusion

Andrew Wiles made significant contributions to algebraic number theory by proving a portion of the Birch and Swinnerton-Dyer conjecture about elliptic curves and the main conjecture of Iwasawa theory about modular forms. During an intensive seven-year period of work he proved a restricted version of the Taniyama-Shimura conjecture for semistable elliptic curves. This result proved Fermat's last theorem, a problem from number theory that mathematicians had been trying to solve for more than three centuries.

FURTHER READING

"Andrew Wiles." Wikipedia, the Free Encyclopedia. Available online. URL: http://en.wikipedia.org/wiki/Andrew_Wiles. Accessed October 31, 2005. Brief online biography with links to other sites and additional explanations.

Coates, John. "Wiles Receives NAS Award in Mathematics." *Notices of the American Mathematical Society* 43, no. 7 (July 1996): 760–763. Summary of Wiles's work on Fermat's last theorem with some biographical information.

Gouvea, Fernando Q. "A Marvelous Proof." *American Mathematical Monthly* 101, no. 3 (March 1994): 203–222. Detailed outline of Wiles's role in the history of the proof of Fermat's last theorem.

Kolata, Gina. "Andrew Wiles: A Math Whiz Battles 350-Year-Old Puzzle." *Math Horizons* (Winter 1993): 8–11. Brief profile of Wiles with insight into his work on Fermat's last theorem. The same article was reprinted as "Andrew Wiles: Quiet Conqueror of a 350-Year-Old Enigma," in *Scientists at Work: Profiles of Today's Groundbreaking Scientists from Science Times*, edited by Laura Chang, 41–47. New York: McGraw-Hill, 2000.

O'Connor, J. J., and E. F. Robertson. "Andrew John Wiles." MacTutor History of Mathematics Archive, University of Saint Andrews. Available online. URL: http://www-groups.dcs.st-andrews.ac.uk/~history/Mathematicians/Wiles.html. Accessed January 27, 2003. Biography provided by the University of Saint Andrews, Scotland.

"The Proof." NOVA Online. Available online. URL: http://www.pbs.org/wgbh/nova/proof. Accessed October 31, 2005. Public Broadcasting System's online site containing an interview with Wiles and a transcript of the October 28, 1997, *NOVA* program by the same name, plus links to pages providing biographical information about Wiles and the history of this famous problem.

Singh, Simon. *Fermat's Enigma: The Epic Quest to Solve the World's Greatest Mathematical Problem.* New York: Walker, 1997. Book about Wiles and other mathematicians who contributed to the solution of Fermat's last theorem.

9

Ingrid Daubechies

(1954–   )

Ingrid Daubechies introduced Daubechies wavelets as an efficient technique for storing and analyzing electronic signals and computer-generated images. *(Denise Applewhite)*

Modeling Images with Wavelets

Ingrid Daubechies (pronounced DOHB-shee) introduced Daubechies wavelets as an easily computed method for representing mathematical functions as sums of basic wave forms. Daubechies wavelets and her subsequent development of biorthogonal wavelets provided researchers with efficient ways to capture electronic signals and digitized images for storing fingerprints, processing images, and analyzing signals. She continues to work with mathematicians, scientists, engineers, and biomedical researchers to develop new applications of wavelets.

Early Life and Education

Ingrid Chantal Daubechies was born on August 17, 1954, in Houthalen, a small mining town in eastern Belgium. Marcel Daubechies, her father, was a civil engineer who worked in the coal mining industry. Simone Daubechies, her mother, held a bachelor's degree in economics, but as the wife of an engineer, she was discouraged from pursuing a career. She later earned a second bachelor's degree in criminology and was employed as a social worker, dealing with children from criminally violent homes. Although her parents spoke both French and Dutch, Ingrid and her brother learned Dutch as their native language. As a child, Ingrid enjoyed weaving, making pottery, reading, and tinkering with machinery. Her early interest in arithmetic was apparent by her awareness of the rule that a number is divisible by nine if the sum of its digits is divisible by nine and by her ability to calculate mentally integer powers of two—$2^1 = 2$, $2^2 = 4$, $2^3 = 8$, $2^4 = 16$, ... At the public elementary and high schools for girls that she attended, she was one of the best students in her mathematics and science classes.

After high school Daubechies enrolled as an undergraduate student at Vrije Universiteit Brussel (VUB; Brussels Free University) in Brussels, Belgium. She chose to major in physics as a compromise between her interest in studying mathematics, her mother's desire for her to become an engineer, and her father's encouragement to become a scientist. The first two years of her focused curriculum included many mathematics courses and no classes in the liberal arts. During her last two years of undergraduate studies, her courses were almost exclusively physics lectures and laboratories. In 1975 she graduated with a bachelor of science degree in physics.

Research in Quantum Physics

For the next five years Daubechies worked to earn her doctoral degree in the Department of Theoretical Physics at VUB. As a graduate research fellow, she spent eight to 10 hours each week conducting problem-solving sessions for students enrolled in undergraduate physics courses. These relatively light teaching duties enabled her to concentrate her efforts on her research in quantum mechanics, the branch of theoretical physics concerned with the analysis of atoms, electrons, and other extremely small particles. Her initial interests were to find functions that described or quantified the movements of subatomic particles. In her first research paper, "An Application of Hyperdifferential Operators to Holomorphic Quantization," which was published in 1978 in the journal *Letters in Mathematical Physics*, she established some topological properties of these quantifying functions and their derivates.

While in graduate school, Daubechies and fellow student Diederik Aerts wrote a series of five research papers about quantum physics applications of Hilbert spaces, mathematical structures in which objects known as vectors can be combined by an inner product operation. One of their joint papers, "Physical Justification for Using the Tensor Product to Describe Two Quantum Systems as One Joint System," was published in 1978 in the Swiss physics journal *Helvetica Physica Acta* (Helvetica physics activities). In this paper they proved that if two physical systems formed the components of a compound system in quantum physics, then the compound system's Hilbert space was the tensor product of the Hilbert spaces of its two subsystems. Their other papers focused on related aspects of the same topic.

Daubechies earned her Ph.D. in physics in 1980 under the direction of Belgian physicist Jean Reignier and French physicist Alexander Grossmann for a dissertation titled "Representation of Quantum Mechanical Operators by Kernels on Hilbert Spaces of Analytic Functions." In her doctoral research she analyzed properties of coherent states, mathematical tools that can be applied to establish a correspondence between quantum mechanics and classical mechanics. Her work involved creating localized functions in a Hilbert space that closely correspond to both the position and the momentum of subatomic particles.

Although she accepted a position at VUB as a research assistant, Daubechies spent the years from 1981 to 1983 on a leave of absence as a postdoctoral research fellow at Princeton University in Princeton, New Jersey, and at New York University's Courant Institute of Mathematical Sciences in New York City. She continued her research on theoretical particle physics and wrote papers individually and in collaboration with several research partners. Typical of her work during this period was her paper "One-Electron Molecules with Relativistic Kinetic Energy: Properties of the Discrete Spectrum," published in 1984 in *Communications in Mathematical Physics*. In this paper she analyzed the eigenvalues and other numerical characteristics of functions that described the behavior of small particles.

In 1984 Daubechies won the Louis Empain Prize for Physics, an award given every five years to a Belgian scientist for scientific contributions completed before the age of 29. Her award-winning paper was titled "Weylkwantisatie bestudeerd via een integraal-transformatie met behulp van het koherentetoestanden-formalisme" (Weyl quantization studied by an integral transformation with the use of the coherent states formalism). In this paper she presented work that extended her dissertation research on the use of functions in a Hilbert space to measure both the position and the momentum of small particles. In the same year she was promoted to the rank of research professor with tenure at VUB.

Between 1984 and 1987 Daubechies collaborated with American mathematical physicist John Klauder to analyze the construction of path integrals, methods for calculating the distance traveled by quantum particles. In their technique they used the path averaging methods introduced earlier by American mathematician Norbert Wiener. They described their joint work in their 1984 paper "Quantum Mechanical Path Integrals with Wiener Measures for All Polynomial Hamiltonians," which was published in *Physical Review Letters*, and their 1985 paper "Quantum Mechanical Path Integrals with Wiener Measures for All Polynomial Hamiltonians II," which appeared in the *Journal of Mathematical Physics*.

Daubechies Wavelets

In 1985 Daubechies started working on the topic of wavelets, elementary mathematical functions that can be used as fundamental building blocks to construct more complicated functions.

As she became interested in this new technique for representing wave forms, she left Belgium to become a member of the technical staff at the Mathematics Research Center at Bell Laboratories in Murray Hill, New Jersey. Her work at Bell Labs focused on developing and analyzing mathematical techniques for signal processing, the branch of applied mathematics concerned with transmitting, manipulating, storing, and reconstructing electrical and electronic signals. During that same year she married A. Robert Calderbank, a British mathematician who also worked at Bell Labs.

The idea of expressing a function as a sum of simpler components had its origins in the work of French mathematician Jean-Baptiste-Joseph Fourier, who pioneered the idea in the early 19th century. His method of Fourier series enabled scientists and engineers to represent sound waves and other periodic functions as infinite sums of basic sine and cosine functions. In 1909 Hungarian mathematician Alfred Haar introduced basic functions now known as Haar wavelets that enabled mathematicians to roughly approximate more complicated functions as sums of short positive and negative pulses. British mathematicians John Littlewood and Raymond Paley improved on this method in the 1930s by grouping frequencies by octaves to represent sound waves. In the 1940s Hungarian mathematician Dennis Gabor introduced the Gabor transform that separated a wave into time-frequency packets. By the 1980s, mathematicians, scientists, and engineers had developed additional techniques to express functions, especially electrical signals and periodic wave forms, as sums of more basic components, but none of their techniques were widely used outside specialized disciplines.

During the 1980s four French scientists developed a systematic general theory of wavelets. Jean Morlet, a geologist trying to improve seismic wave techniques for detecting underground oil reserves, developed the concepts of wavelets of constant shape, fundamental functions that retained their shape when they were shifted, stretched, or reduced. In 1984 Grossmann and Morlet confirmed that functions could be decomposed into wavelets of constant shape and then reconstructed into smooth signals, even if small errors of measurement or computation had occurred. Physicist Yves Meyer improved on their work by introducing systems of wavelets that were orthogonal, meaning that each wavelet represented information that was independent of the information captured by all other wavelets. In 1986 computer scientist Stéphane Mallat reduced the process of computing wavelets to a simple calculation of averages and differences of small portions of each signal.

During February and March of 1987 Daubechies developed a new theory of compactly supported, orthonormal wavelets, now known as Daubechies wavelets. The quality of compact support meant that each wavelet took nonzero values only on a finite interval. Orthonormality meant that each wavelet independently represented a different aspect of the function being modeled and that the wavelets were all of a uniform size. She introduced her ideas in a conference presentation titled "Orthonormal Bases of Wavelets with Finite Support—Connections with Discrete Filters" that she presented at the 1987 International Workshop on Wavelets and Applications in Marseille, France. Her 87-page paper "Orthonormal Bases of Compactly Supported Wavelets," which was published in 1988 in the journal *Communications on Pure and Applied Mathematics*, provided a more thorough explanation of her new theory. This paper made wavelets readily available to a broad

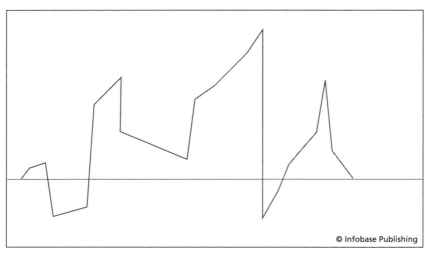

© Infobase Publishing

A typical Daubechies wavelet is an irregularly shaped curve with rough edges and frequent spikes. A sound wave can be efficiently reproduced by adding a collection of these basic curves that each capture different features of the original wave.

audience of mathematicians, scientists, and engineers for a wide range of applications.

Daubechies's new class of wavelets had many desirable properties that made them more useful than all prior variations of wavelets. They were easily implemented on computers using simple, well-known techniques of digital filtering. Although each wavelet was a jagged curve with irregular edges the signal produced by the sum of a collection of Daubechies wavelets was smooth. Because they were an orthonormal set of waves, they efficiently captured the characteristics of the wave being modeled without any redundancy. As a compactly supported function, each Daubechies wavelet represented information from a small section of the larger function in a simpler way than the basic functions did in more cumbersome techniques such as windowed Fourier transforms.

At the end of her landmark 1988 paper, Daubechies included a table of coefficients that provided explicit information about expressing a function as a sum of its Daubechies wavelets. This practical information allowed engineers to begin applying immediately her ideas to the processing of digitized electronic signals. They were able to compress all the characteristics of a wave form into a discrete set of coefficients that provided instructions on how to reconstruct the curve from scaled and shifted copies of a "father" wavelet. Daubechies wavelets rapidly became fundamental tools for signal processing.

Digital Image Compression

During the 1990s Daubechies made a transition from an industrial environment back to an academic setting. Although she remained on the technical staff at Bell Labs until 1994, she spent a six-month leave of absence at the University of Michigan in 1990, and from 1991 to 1993 she taught as a professor in the Department of Mathematics at Rutgers University in New Brunswick, New Jersey. In 1992 she published the book *Ten Lectures on Wavelets* that provided a review of the most recent developments in the theory of wavelets and a tutorial explaining how to apply the theory to practical problems in signal processing, image processing, and numerical analysis. This book won the 1994 Leroy P. Steele Prize for Mathematical Exposition from the American Mathematical Society (AMS) and immediately became recognized as the standard reference work on the subject of wavelets.

Traveling around the United States, Daubechies gave lectures on wavelets to diverse audiences of mathematicans and scientists. In an invited address at the joint annual meetings of the AMS, the Mathematical Association of America (MAA), and the Society for Industrial and Applied Mathematics (SIAM) in Baltimore, Maryland, in January 1992, she presented a lecture titled "Wavelets Making Waves in Mathematics and Engineering." The AMS published the videotape of this presentation on the history of wavelets as part of its series *Selected Lectures in Mathematics*. At the 1992 Frontiers of Science symposium sponsored by the National Academy of Science (NAS), she explained how wavelets were used to represent, transmit, and reconstruct electronic waves in a paper titled "Wavelets and Signal Analysis." Daubechies explained additional applications of wavelets in her June 1992 lecture "Wavelets: A Tool for Time-Frequency Analysis" that she delivered at the Spring Meeting of the Northeastern Section of the MAA at Merrimack College in North Andover, Massachusetts, and in her presentation titled "Wavelet Transforms and Orthonormal Wavelet Bases" at the 1993 AMS conference "Different Perspectives on Wavelets" in San Antonio, Texas.

Daubechies developed additional techniques that expanded the applications of wavelets. With French mathematicians Albert Cohen and Jean-Christophe Feauveau she coauthored the paper "Biorthogonal Bases of Compactly Supported Wavelets," which was published in 1992 in the journal *Communications on Pure and Applied Mathematics*. In this paper they introduced a technique that used two sets of mutually orthogonal wave forms to represent two-dimensional images, one set for decomposition and the other for reconstruction of the image. Within a year, researchers at the Federal Bureau of Investigation (FBI) and the Los Alamos National Laboratory used this technique to develop a method for digitally storing and matching fingerprints. The wavelet scalar quantization (WSQ) method allows images of fingerprints to be compressed at a 20-to-one ratio without any significant loss of image detail. In 1993 the FBI adopted this method to store and match their database of

200 million fingerprints and achieved a savings of 93 percent in the space required to store the information.

In the biomedical field, researchers use Daubechies's techniques to process and analyze signals from imaging devices such as electrocardiograms (EKGs), electroencephalograms (EEGs), and magnetic resonance images (MRIs). Because wavelets are not compromised by corruptions in the acquisition or transmission of small amounts of data, wavelet-based images provide more reliable representations of the anatomical region being scanned. Additionally, wavelet-based images can be more efficiently analyzed for evidence of abnormalities or disease because their more efficient representation requires the processing of less information.

The biorthogonal bases introduced by Daubechies, Cohen, and Feauveau have become the most commonly used wavelets for image processing. In addition to their uses in biomedicine and fingerprinting analysis, researchers in other fields use Daubechies wavelets and biorthogonal wavelets to find meaningful patterns in turbulent systems such as the flow of air around the wing of an airplane, the path of electrically charged gases in a nuclear reactor, and the flow of water through a network of pipes. Geologists employ wavelet-based images of sound waves traveling through layers of rock to analyze the composition of the material and detect layers of coal, salt, or oil. Filmmakers use wavelets in the computer animation of cartoon characters. Musical researchers employ wavelets to identify and remove static from imperfect recordings. Wavelets allowed researchers in the image processing field to introduce new standards in 2000 for storing digital images as JPEG files.

The broad impact of her research on wavelets earned Daubechies widespread recognition. In 1992 she received a John D. and Catherine T. MacArthur Fellowship, an award of $60,000 per year to fund her travel and research activities for a period of five years. The following year the American Academy of Arts and Sciences elected her as a fellow. In 1997 the AMS awarded her the Ruth Lyttle Satter Prize in Mathematics in recognition of her pioneering work with wavelets and their applications. The NAS inducted her as a member in 1998 and presented her the NAS Award in Mathematics in 2000. In 1998 the Institute of Electrical and Electronics Engineers (IEEE) elected her as a fellow and awarded her the IEEE Information Theory Society Golden Jubilee Award for Technological Innovation. Daubechies received the 1998 International Society for Optical Engineering Recognition of Outstanding Achievement and was elected a foreign member of Royal Netherlands Academy of Arts and Sciences in 1999. The Eduard Rhein Foundation honored her with its 2000 Basic Research Award for the invention, mathematical advancement, and application of wavelets. The MAA named her its 2001 Earle Raymond Hedrick Lecturer.

Continued Research on Wave Representations

Daubechies, and French mathematicians Stéphane Jaffard and Jean-Lin Journe developed a new tool for analyzing waves that combined some of the advantages of wavelets with some of the strengths of Fourier series. In their 1991 paper "A Simple Wilson Orthonormal Basis with Exponential Decay," published in the *SIAM Journal on Mathematical Analysis*, they introduced a collection of orthonormal basis functions involving sines and cosines that are damped so that their values diminish with time. Their method quickly became a standard tool for time frequency analysis and for the numerical analysis of partial differential equations, equations involving the derivates of functions of several variables.

In 1994 she joined the faculty at Princeton University in Princeton, New Jersey, as a professor in the mathematics department and in the university's Program in Applied and Computational Mathematics (PACM). From 1997 to 2001 she directed the PACM, which provides intensive training in applied mathematics to a select group of undergraduate and graduate students. Since 2004 she has held an endowed chair as Princeton's William R. Kenan, Jr., Professor. At Princeton she teaches undergraduate and graduate courses, directs the research of doctoral students, and collaborates with postdoctoral research fellows and her colleagues. She has also helped create curriculum materials that reflect current applications of mathematics for students in kindergarten through grade 12.

Through her recent and current research Daubechies has been working to extend the applications of wavelets to new areas. In 1996 she and IBM scientist Stéphane Maes coauthored a chapter titled "A Nonlinear Squeezing of the Continuous Wavelet Transform Based on Auditory Nerve Models" for the book *Wavelets in Medicine and Biology.* Their joint work applied wavelet techniques to model the human process of hearing. In 2002 Daubechies and Cohen collaborated with electrical engineer Onur Guleryuz from Brooklyn's Polytechnic University and Michael Orchard from Rice University to cowrite the paper "On the Importance of Combining Wavelet-Based Nonlinear Approximation with Coding Strategies," which was published in the *IEEE Transactions on Information Theory.* Their article explained the advantages and disadvantages of using only a limited number of the largest coefficients of the wavelet expansion for a digital signal that is transmitting data. With mathematician Bin Han from the University of Alberta, computer scientist Amos Ron from the University of Wisconsin-Madison, and mathematician Zuowei Shen from the University of Singapore she coauthored a paper titled "Framelets: MRA-Based Constructions of Wavelet Frames," which appeared in 2004 in the journal *Applied and Computational Harmonic Analysis.* In this paper the four researchers explained how framelets—the individual elements of certain types of wavelet systems—provide methods for conducting multiresolution analysis (MRA). Other engineers and scientists are attempting to build on Daubechies's work to analyze shock waves produced by explosions, to encode multiple signals traveling through a single transmission line, and to develop better systems for predicting the weather.

In addition to writing more than 100 research papers on quantum mechanics and wavelets and directing students' doctoral research, Daubechies has served the mathematical community through her work for journals, committees, and professional societies. As coeditor in chief of the journal *Applied and Computational Harmonic Analysis* and as a member of the editorial boards of 10 other journals, she reviews the work of mathematical and scientific researchers and helps set the direction for future research. Daubechies served as a member of the United States National Committee on Mathematics and the European Mathematical Society's Commission on the Applications of Mathematics. She is a member of five professional societies: the AMS, MAA, SIAM, IEEE, and the Association for Women in Mathematics.

Conclusion

Ingrid Daubechies's introduction of the concept of compactly supported orthonormal wavelets, known as Daubechies wavelets, provided an accessible computational tool for signal and image processing. Her landmark paper and her classic book have become two of the most frequently referenced works on the subject. Daubechies wavelets and her subsequent introduction of biorthogonal wavelets made possible the efficient storage, manipulation, and analysis of fingerprints, animated images, electronic signals, biomedical images, seismic waves, and musical recordings.

FURTHER READING

Haunsperger, Deanna, and Stephen Kennedy. "Coal Miner's Daughter." *Math Horizons*, April 2000, pp. 5–8, 28–30. Article with both biographical and mathematical content for an undergraduate audience.

Jacquez, Kelley Reynolds. "Ingrid Daubechies, 1954– , Belgium-born American Applied Mathematician and Educator." In *Notable Mathematicians: From Ancient Times to the Present*, edited by Robyn V. Young, 137–138. Detroit, Mich.: Gale, 1998. Brief but informative profile of Daubechies and her work.

Kort, Edith. "Ingrid Daubechies." In *Notable Women in Mathematics: A Biographical Dictionary*, edited by Charlene Morrow and Teri Perl, 34–38. Westport, Conn.: Greenwood Press, 1998. Short biography of Daubechies.

Mackenzie, Dana. "Wavelets: Seeing the Forest and the Trees." Beyond Discovery, National Academy of Science. Available online. URL: http://www.beyonddiscovery.org/content/view. article.asp?a=1952. Accessed November 11, 2005. Detailed online article about the development and applications of wavelets, with a link to an audio interview with Daubechies.

O'Connor, J. J., and E. F. Robertson. "Ingrid Daubechies." MacTutor History of Mathematics Archive, University of Saint Andrews. Available online. URL: http://www-groups.dcs.st-andrews.ac.uk/~history/Mathematicians/Daubechies.html. Accessed March 14, 2003. Biography provided by the University of Saint Andrews, Scotland.

Perrault, Anne Marie. "Ingrid Daubechies (1954–), Physicist." In *Notable Women in the Physical Sciences*, edited by Benjamin F. Shearer and Barbara S. Shearer, 67–69. Westport, Conn.: Greenwood Press, 1997. Brief profile of Daubechies and her work with wavelets.

Riddle, Larry. "Ingrid Daubechies." Agnes Scott College. Available online. URL: http://www.agnesscott.edu/lriddle/women/daub. htm. Accessed March 17, 2003. Brief biography with several links and references.

Von Baeyer, Hans Christian. "Wave of the Future." *Discover*, May 1995, pp. 68–75. Article in popular magazine providing a description of Daubechies's work on wavelets with some biographical information.

Sarah Flannery

(1982–   )

Sarah Flannery developed an efficient algorithm for encrypting messages. *(Sion Touhig/CORBIS SYGMA)*

New Algorithm for Cryptography

As a 16-year-old high school student, Sarah Flannery developed a new algorithm for encoding and decoding digital messages. In her project that won national and international science competitions, she demonstrated that her technique was faster than the industry standard RSA cryptosystem. She works as a researcher developing mathematical software.

Solving Puzzles

Sarah Flannery was born on January 31, 1982, in the village of Blarney in County Cork, Ireland, to David Flannery, a mathematician, and Sarah Flannery, a biologist. She and her four younger brothers, Michael, Brian, David, and Eamonn, grew up on a rural dairy farm five miles from Cork Institute of Technology (CIT), where her father was a professor in the mathematics department and her mother was a part-time microbiology lecturer. She obtained the first six years of her education at the local primary school for girls and spent the next six years at Scoil Mhuire gan Smál (School of Mary the Immaculate), a coeducational secondary school in Blarney.

During her childhood Flannery's father challenged her and her brothers to solve puzzles on a chalkboard that hung in the family's kitchen. One classic puzzle that she solved at the age of five involved using a five-gallon jug and a three-gallon jug to measure out four gallons of water. Another puzzle asked how long it would take a rabbit to climb out of a hole 30 meters deep if it climbed up three meters each day and slipped back two meters each night. Other puzzles involved a farmer transporting a lion, a goat, and a cabbage across a river, a fly flying back and forth between two approaching trains, a monk climbing up and down a mountain, and three runners competing in a race.

One particular puzzle whose solution typified the reasoning processes that Flannery employed was the construction of all the 3×3 magic squares for the numbers 1, 2, 3, . . . , 9. In order to solve this puzzle, one needs to insert the integers from 1 through 9 into a grid of squares arranged into three rows and three columns so that each row, each column, and each diagonal produces the same sum. Rather than sift through the 362,880 possible ways to arrange the numbers in the grid of nine squares, Flannery reasoned logically that there were only eight solutions and that they were all simple variations of a single solution. Since each number must occur exactly once in the matrix, she reasoned that the sum of all three rows is $1 + 2 + 3 + . . . + 9 = 45$. She concluded that the sum of each row, column, and diagonal must be 15 and generated the eight different combinations of three numbers that summed to that common total. Flannery

2	9	4
7	5	3
6	1	8

One of the mathematical puzzles Flannery's father asked her and her brothers to solve was to place the digits 1, 2, 3, . . . , 9 into an array of squares arranged into a 3 × 3 grid so that each row, each column, and each diagonal produces the same sum. This arrangement is one of eight solutions of the 3 × 3 magic square.

observed that the entry in the center of the magic square must be 5 because the value in this position will be involved in four sums (one row, one column, and two diagonals), and 5 is the only number having this property. Since each of the even numbers, 2, 4, 6, and 8, can be included in three sums that add up to 15 while each of the odd numbers, 1, 3, 7, and 9, can be included in only two such sums, she reasoned that the even numbers must occupy the corners of the magic square while the odd numbers must be placed in the four remaining noncorner positions. She completed her analysis by noticing that four of the eight resulting magic squares were the same arrangement of numbers rotated a quarter of a turn from each other and that the final four solutions could be obtained by flipping the first four.

Successfully wrestling with the logic and mathematics of the magic square and other puzzles helped Flannery develop strong skills in problem solving and abstract thinking. Talking her way through multiple strategies and developing creative solution methods increased her confidence in her ability to take on challenges. In addition to solving puzzles, Flannery maintained interests in team sports such as basketball, Gaelic football, cross-country running, and hurling and in individual activities including boating, playing the piano, and playing the tin whistle. An avid horseback rider, she participated in show jumping competitions with her horse Clydie.

Cryptography Project for Science Fair

As a 10th-grade student in 1997, Flannery decided to participate in a transition year—an optional year of project-based learning with no examinations—before completing her final two years of high school. She and her classmates established a business to manufacture and sell Christmas cards and decorations, sold shares in the company, marketed their products, generated a profit, and dissolved the company. During a trip to an outdoor education center her group learned survival techniques, orienteering, and rappelling. In another project she organized and participated in a fashion show after taking a professional modeling course. Pursuing her interest in mathematics she enrolled in a Saturday morning program for advanced high school students titled "Enrichment Course in Mathematics" at University College Cork (UCC). One evening each week she also attended her father's noncredit course "Mathematical Excursions" at CIT in which she explored ideas in higher-level mathematics.

Flannery's most time-consuming activity during her transition year was her science fair project on cryptography, the study of coding and decoding messages. Combining ideas she learned from her father's course with information she obtained through her independent research, she developed a project that explained the terminology and basic ideas of classical and modern cryptosystems. She explained methods that ranged from the Caesar cipher that Roman military officers had used 2,000 years ago to public key cryptography, a collection of techniques developed in the late 20th century that allow the sender to make public the process used to encrypt a message without revealing how to decrypt it. Using the software package Mathematica, she implemented several cryptographical methods on laptop computers to demonstrate the process of encrypting messages from plaintext to ciphertext and decrypting the coded ciphertext back to the original message.

In January 1998 Flannery traveled to the Royal Dublin Society in Ballsbridge, Dublin, to participate in the Esat Young Scientist and Technology Exhibition, the national science fair sponsored by the Irish telecommunications and Internet company Esat Telecommunication Limited. Her entry, "Cryptography—The Science of Secrecy," earned first place in the Individual Intermediate Mathematics, Physics, and Chemistry category, won a Display Award for the same section, and received the Intel Excellence Award. As the winner of the Intel prize, she gave a short talk on cryptography to her Saturday morning classmates at UCC and became Ireland's representative at the Intel International Science and Engineering Fair (ISEF), held in May in Fort Worth, Texas, under the sponsorship of the computer manufacturer Intel Corporation.

Cayley-Purser Cryptography Algorithm

In April 1998 Flannery spent a one-week internship at Baltimore Technologies, a Dublin-based data security company, to fulfill another requirement of her transition year of high school. William Whyte, Baltimore's senior cryptologist, gave her an unpublished paper written by Michael Purser, the company's founder and head cryptographer. In the paper Purser had proposed a method for encrypting digital signatures using quaternions, a four-dimensional generalization of complex numbers. Within three days Flannery mastered the advanced undergraduate-level mathematics that formed the theoretical basis of the algorithm and produced a working implementation of the system.

After completing her internship, Flannery developed Purser's ideas into a cryptographical scheme using 2×2 matrices of non-negative integers. Her method was based on the selection of two large prime numbers, p and q, each at least 100 digits in length, and the calculation of their product $n = p \cdot q$. All arithmetic was performed modulo n, meaning that the result of each computation was adjusted to a corresponding integer value between 0 and $n - 1$. After identifying a pair of matrices, A and C for which $A \cdot C \neq C \cdot A$, she calculated matrices B, D, E, G, and K that played various roles in the algorithm. For each 2×2 matrix P whose entries represented four letters of the plaintext message, her algorithm produced the encrypted ciphertext matrix $S = K \cdot P \cdot K$. When the sender transmitted the collection of ciphertext matrices and the auxiliary matrix E, the receiver could form the deciphering key L by combining matrices E and C and then decipher each ciphertext matrix by the simple operation $P = L \cdot S \cdot L$.

Flannery's algorithm differed in a fundamental way from the RSA algorithm, the commercial public-key cryptosystem that is used on 300 million computer systems worldwide. Cryptologists Ronald Rivest, Adi Shamir, and Leonard Adleman had invented the RSA method in 1977 when they were students at the Massachusetts Institute of Technology (MIT) in Cambridge. Their technique is also based on the product of two large primes but uses exponentiation rather than matrix multiplication to encode and decode messages. After calculating the products $n = p \cdot q$ and $m = (p - 1) \cdot (q - 1)$, the three men determined two positive integers c and d for which $c \cdot d = 1$ modulo m, meaning that $c \cdot d = 1 + m \cdot k$ for some integer k. For each 2×2 plaintext matrix P, their algorithm produced the encrypted ciphertext matrix $S = P^c$ through the process of exponentiation, or repeated multiplication. The receiver could decrypt each ciphertext matrix by performing the operation $P = S^d$. Both algorithms derived their strength from the difficulty of factoring the 200-digit number n into a product of large primes.

To fully implement her algorithm, Flannery read articles from scholarly journals about advanced techniques for factoring and extracting roots of matrices, methods for finding inverses of matrices, properties of modular arithmetic, and mathematical structures known as groups, rings, and finite fields. Using the mathematical software package Mathematica, she wrote computer programs to implement her algorithm and the RSA algorithm. When she ran both programs to encrypt and decrypt 12 copies of German-American poet Max Ehrmann's poem "Desiderata" and compared the execution times, she discovered that her algorithm ran faster. Although her encryption key and her ciphertext were about eight times as long as those produced by the RSA algorithm, incorporating the process of matrix multiplication rather than matrix exponentiation significantly reduced the amount of computations required.

She was not able to prove that her algorithm was secure—that messages encoded using her algorithm could not be decoded without knowing the decryption matrix—but it did survive the variety of attacks that she attempted.

At the weeklong ISEF fair in May 1998, Flannery's revised project won a third-place Karl Menger Memorial Award from the American Mathematical Society (AMS), a fourth-place Grand Award in the mathematics category, and the prestigious $2,000 Intel Fellows Achievement Award. After the fair, she named her algorithm the Cayley-Purser (CP) algorithm in honor of Arthur Cayley, the 19th-century English mathematician who developed the algebra of matrices, and Michael Purser, whose quaternion-based cryptographical scheme she adapted for 2×2 matrices.

Ireland's Young Scientist of the Year

In the fall of 1998 Flannery took her father's "Mathematical Excursions" course again and made additional revisions to her CP algorithm. She improved her computer programs and ran both the CP and RSA algorithms for moduli ranging in size from 200-digit to 300-digit integers. Her program executions revealed that CP was 22 to 30 times faster than RSA. When she presented her project and a 50-page report titled "Cryptography—A New Algorithm Versus the RSA" at the January 1999 Esat Telecom Young Scientist and Technology Exhibition, she won first place in the physics, chemistry, and mathematics category; was honored as the competition's overall winner; and was named Ireland's Young Scientist of the Year for 1999. At the awards ceremony, Bertie Ahern, Ireland's *taoiseach* (prime minister), presented her with a silver trophy and an award of 1,000 Irish pounds (approximately $1,400). Her first-place finish earned her a one-week trip to Thessaloníki, Greece, to represent Ireland at the European Union Contest for Young Scientists in September.

Flannery's achievement generated much publicity and brought her widespread recognition. During the next three weeks she sat for 300 interviews with reporters from local, national, and international newspapers, magazines, radio stations, and television programs. The lord mayor of Cork named her Cork Person of the Month, she met with Irish president Mary McAlese, and the organizers of the information technology exhibition IT@Cork presented her with a laptop computer. Although she rejected a lucrative offer to appear in an advertisement for Pepsi-Cola, Flannery permitted the promotion company for the Spice Girls singing group to include in their fan magazine an article about her titled "Smart Spice—Pop Babes Think Irish Whizzkid Has Girl Power." Some media reports proclaimed her a genius and predicted that she would become rich when her new algorithm was implemented by banks, businesses, and governmental agencies. After lengthy consideration she turned down numerous offers of college scholarships and business partnerships and decided not to seek a patent for her algorithm.

Flannery declined invitations to lecture about the CP algorithm at math department seminars and meetings of student math and computer clubs at numerous colleges and universities but did accept three speaking engagements. She traveled to Singapore to speak at the closing ceremony of the National Science Talent Search Contest and to give four talks to groups of high school students. At a leadership conference for women in Milan, Italy, sponsored by International Business Machines (IBM), she described her project to an international audience of 200 executives. Her final speaking engagement was at the annual meeting of the Dublin Mathematics Teachers' Association at St. Patrick's College in Drumcondra, Dublin.

The publicity generated by the media reports focused scrutiny on the security of Flannery's algorithm. Although she had successfully tested her algorithm against several types of attacks, it had not undergone the extensive peer review process required to establish an encryption scheme as being satisfactorily secure. After reading her report, a mathematician who specializes in cryptography identified a crucial flaw that enables a person to use the publicly available portions of the algorithm to create a matrix that will decrypt the ciphertext. Flannery, Purser, and Whyte analyzed the breach and concluded that it was not possible to patch the defect. The CP algorithm was an effective private key algorithm, but it could not be classified as a public key cryptosystem.

Flannery spent four weeks in July and August at the Smart Card Division of IBM Development Laboratories in Böblingen, Germany. During this internship she used the Java programming language to program smart cards, plastic cards similar to credit cards containing microprocessor chips that enable the cards to store information and modify that information during transactions. These cards that have been used in the telephone, transportation, banking, and health care industries incorporate more sophisticated security features than cards that use the simpler technology of magnetic strips.

In September Flannery displayed her project at the 1999 European Union Young Scientist Contest in Thessaloníki. Her condensed 10-page report, titled "Cryptography: An Investigation of a New Algorithm Versus the RSA," compared the design and performance of the two algorithms and included an appendix explaining the mathematical deficiency that made her CP algorithm insecure as a public key cryptosystem. She won one of three first prizes, was named European Young Scientist of the Year 1999, and received an award of 5,000 euros (worth approximately $6,000). With the other winners of the competition she spent a week in December in Stockholm, Sweden, attending the Nobel Prize ceremonies and participating in the Youth Science Seminar.

College and Professional Life

After graduating from high school in 2000, Flannery enrolled as a computer science major at Peterhouse College of Cambridge University in Cambridge, England. In addition to completing her academic work, she cowrote a book with her father about her experiences with the CP algorithm and the four science fairs. The book, *In Code—A Mathematical Journey*, also discussed some of the puzzles she had solved and the basic mathematics involved in cryptography. During the summer of 2001 the release of the American edition of the book took her on a lecture tour of eight cities around the United States.

In 2003 Flannery earned her bachelor's degree in computer science from Cambridge and accepted a position as a research associate in the Scientific Information Group at Wolfram Research, the company that produces the Mathematica software package. She participated in the 2003 NKS Summer School, a program for young scientists sponsored by Steven Wolfram, the author of the book *A New Kind of Science* and the founder of Wolfram Research.

During this summer program for talented young scientists, she completed a project titled "An Investigation of Cellular Automaton Rule Number 699927 and Other Distractions!" in which she investigated patterns produced in a rectangular grid of cells by repeated application of simple rules involving the states of neighboring cells.

As a research associate at Wolfram, Flannery works on the development of technical computing software and coordinates the company's educational outreach programs. In August 2005 she presented a lecture titled "Exploring Mathematics and Science with Mathematica" at Macquarie University in Sydney, Australia. During the Wolfram Research Tour of Ireland and Northern Ireland, she gave a series of presentations in November 2005 titled "Using Mathematica in Teaching and Research."

Conclusion

Sarah Flannery won national and international science competitions for developing and analyzing the Cayley-Purser cryptographic algorithm. She demonstrated that her method of encoding and decoding data was more than 20 times faster than RSA, the leading commercial public key cryptosystem, and explained the underlying mathematical reasons that make it vulnerable to attacks. A graduate of Cambridge University, she develops mathematical software for Wolfram Research.

FURTHER READING

Abbey, Cherrie D. "Sarah Flannery." In *Biography Today: Scientists and Inventors Series*, vol. 5, 53–63. Detroit, Mich.: Omnigraphics, 2001. Biographical sketch of Flannery with description of her work, geared toward young readers.

Flannery, Sarah, with David Flannery. *In Code: A Mathematical Journey*. New York: Workman, 2001. Autobiographical book describing Flannery's life and her development of the prize-winning coding scheme. The American edition includes 100 more pages and more mathematics than the original United Kingdom edition, published by Profile Books.

Schaefer, Marvin. "'In Code: A Mathematical Journey' by Sarah Flannery with David Flannery, Reviewed by Marvin Schaefer." Read This! The MAA Online Book Review Column. Available online. URL: http://www.maa.org/reviews/incode.html. Accessed June 7, 2004. Thorough book review on the Mathematical Association of America Web site, providing biographical information and a description of Flannery's algorithm.

Weisstein, Eric W., et al. "Cayley-Purser Algorithm." *MathWorld—* A Wolfram Web Resource. Available online. URL: http://math world.wolfram.com/Cayley-PurserAlgorithm.html. Accessed November 4, 2005. Explanation of Flannery's encryption algorithm.

GLOSSARY

algebra   The branch of mathematics dealing with the manipulation of variables and equations.

algebraic equation   A mathematical statement equating two algebraic expressions.

algebraic expression   An expression built up out of numbers and variables using the operations of addition, subtraction, multiplication, division, raising to a power, and taking a root.

algebraic geometry   The branch of mathematics concerned with the study of the roots of polynomial equations.

algebraic number theory   The branch of mathematics that employs algebraic technique to investigate properties of the integers.

algebraic topology   The branch of mathematics in which groups of functions are used to study the properties of geometrical surfaces.

algebraic variety   A surface defined by a polynomial equation in a higher-dimensional space.

algorithm   A precise set of instructions for solving a problem.

arithmetic   The study of computation.

astronomy   The scientific study of stars, planets, and other heavenly bodies.

axiom   A statement giving a property of an undefined term or a relationship between undefined terms. The axioms of a specific mathematical theory govern the behavior of the undefined terms in that theory; they are assumed to be true and cannot be proved. Also known as a postulate.

big bang theory   The theory in physics that asserts that the universe began with the explosion of a black hole.

bipartite graphs A graph in which the vertices are partitioned into two sets so that every edge joins a node from one set with a node from the other.

black hole A dense concentration of mass so great that its gravitational field prevents any mass or energy, including light, from escaping.

Brouwer fixed-point theorem The principle from algebraic topology that any continuous function on the surface of an n-dimensional sphere must map at least one point back into itself.

buckyball A polyhedron constructed from 20 hexagons and 12 pentagons.

Calabi conjecture A question, suggested by Eugenio Calabi and solved by Shing-Tung Yau, concerning how volume and distance can be measured for certain types of surfaces in five or more dimensions.

calculus The branch of mathematics dealing with derivatives and integrals.

cardinality A numerical value giving the size of a set.

Cayley-Purser A cryptographic algorithm created by Sarah Flannery that uses the multiplication of 2×2 matrices to code and decode messages.

celestial mechanics The branch of physics dealing with the motion of heavenly bodies.

cellular automata The generation of patterns on grids of cells according to a set of rules concerning the status of a cell and its neighbors.

circle The set of all points in a plane at a given distance (the radius) from a fixed point (the center).

coding theory The analysis of methods for manipulating and transmitting blocks of data.

coefficient A number or known quantity that multiplies a variable in an algebraic expression.

coherent states Mathematical tools that can be applied to establish a correspondence between quantum mechanics and classical mechanics.

combinatorics The branch of mathematics concerned with the study of counting techniques.

complete graphs A graph in which every pair of vertices is connected by an edge.

complex number A number that can be written as the sum of a real number and the square root of a negative real number.

computer program A set of instructions that controls the operation of a computer.

conjecture A mathematical statement that has been proposed but not yet proved.

Conway groups Three large finite groups—Co_1, Co_2, and Co_3—discovered by John Conway.

Conway polynomial A polynomial introduced by John Conway whose algebraic properties correspond to the geometric properties of the associated knot.

Conway's knot A particular knot introduced by John Conway that has 11 crossings and cannot be produced from a combination of simpler knots.

coordinates The numbers indicating the location of a point on a plane or in a higher-dimensional space.

cosine For an acute angle in a right triangle, the ratio of the adjacent side to the hypotenuse.

cosmology The branch of physics concerned with the study of the origin and evolution of the universe.

countable An infinite set is countable if it can be put into a one-to-one correspondence with the set of natural numbers.

cryptography The study of coding and decoding secret messages.

cube (1) A regular solid having six congruent faces, each of which is a square. (2) To multiply a quantity times itself three times; raise to the third power.

cubic (1) A polynomial of degree 3. (2) An equation or curve (graph) corresponding to a cubic polynomial.

Daubechies wavelets Compactly supported orthonormal wavelets introduced by Ingrid Daubechies to efficiently represent signals and images as sums of irregular but basic wave forms.

decidable A set of numbers such as the integers or real numbers is decidable if there exists a single algorithm capable of deciding the truth of every statement involving addition, multiplication, elementary logic, and variables representing numbers in this set.

decryption The process of translating a coded message from ciphertext to plaintext.

degree (1) A unit of angle measure equal to $\dfrac{1}{360}$ of a circle. (2) The number of edges that meet at a vertex in a polygon or polyhedron. (3) The sum of the exponents of all the variables occurring in a term of a polynomial or algebraic expression.

degree of a polynomial or equation The highest exponent occurring in any of its terms.

derivative A function formed as the limit of a ratio of differences of the values of another function. One of two fundamental ideas of calculus that indicates the rate at which a quantity is changing.

diagonal In a square or a rectangle, the line joining two opposite corners.

differential equation An equation involving derivatives.

differential geometry The branch of mathematics that uses derivatives and integrals to describe and analyze geometrical objects such as surfaces in higher-dimensional spaces.

differentiation The process of determining the derivative of a function.

Diophantine analysis The area of number theory dealing with methods for finding integer solutions of equations (usually involving polynomials) with integer coefficients.

divisible A number is divisible by another if the resulting quotient has no remainder.

elliptic curve An equation of the form $y^2 = x^3 + ax^2 + bx + c$, where the coefficients a, b, and c are integers.

encryption The process of translating a message into a secret code.

equation A mathematical sentence stating that two algebraic expressions or numerical quantities have the same value.

event horizon The boundary of a black hole beyond which no electromagnetic energy can travel.

existential definability A set of positive integers is existentially definable if a parameter in a solvable Diophantine equation generates all the values in the set.

exponent   A number indicating how many repeated factors of the quantity occur. Also known as power.

exponentiation   The process of raising a quantity to a power.

factor   An integer that divides a given integer without leaving a remainder.

Fermat's last theorem   A principle in number theory conjectured by Pierre de Fermat stating that there are no positive integers x, y, and z that satisfy the equation $x^n + y^n = z^n$ for any integer $n > 2$.

Fibonacci numbers   A sequence of integers beginning 1, 1, 2, 3, 5, 8, 13, 21, . . . in which each number is the sum of the two numbers immediately preceding it.

finite group   A set with finitely many elements that satisfy four algebraic properties.

Fourier series   An infinite series whose terms are of the form a_n $\sin(nx)$ and $b_n \cos(nx)$.

fraction   See RATIONAL NUMBER.

framelets   The individual elements of certain wavelet systems.

Game of Life   See LIFE.

game theory   The branch of mathematics dealing with the study of competition and cooperation.

gamma rays   High-energy, potentially harmful radiation generated in nuclear reactions that penetrate through certain materials.

general theory of relativity   Theory from physics that explains the laws of gravity and the behavior of the universe at large.

geometry   The mathematical study of shapes, forms, their transformations, and the spaces that contain them.

graph   (1) A collection of points or vertices that are connected to one another by line segments called edges. (2) A picture of all the points whose coordinates satisfy a given equation.

graph theory   The branch of mathematics in which relationships between objects are represented by a collection of vertices and edges.

gravitation   The attractive force that pulls objects toward each other.

group   A set of objects that can be combined with an operation that satisfies four basic conditions.

group theory   The branch of abstract algebra dealing with the structure, properties, and interaction of groups.

Hawking radiation   Theoretical radiation emitted by black holes according to a theory introduced by Stephen Hawking.

Hilbert's 10th problem   One of 23 questions posed by David Hilbert in 1900, it asks if it is possible to create a single algorithm that will determine if any given Diophantine equation has integer solutions.

hydrodynamics   The branch of physics dealing with the study of the properties of fluids in motion.

information paradox   Controversial concept in physics asserting that information about the matter and energy that formed a black hole is irretrievably lost when the black hole collapses.

integer   A whole number such as –4, –1, 0, 2, or 5.

integral   A function formed as the limit of a sum of terms defined by another function. One of two fundamental ideas of calculus that can be used to find the area under a curve.

integration   The process of determining the integral of a function.

irrational number   A real number such as $\sqrt{2}$ or π that cannot be expressed as a ratio of two integers.

isometric imbedding   A map from a manifold to a higher-dimensional space that preserves the distances between corresponding pairs of points in both spaces.

Iwasawa theory   An area of number theory that uses techniques introduced by Kenkichi Iwasawa to establish connections between the structures of collections of numbers and related collections of functions that are known as algebraic number fields and algebraic function fields, respectively.

knot theory   The mathematical study of the properties of knots.

Langlands program   An effort initiated in the 1960s by Robert Langlands to establish unifying connections between seemingly unrelated branches of mathematics.

lattice   (1) A regular geometrical arrangement of points in the plane. (2) The fundamental four-sided region of the plane corresponding to an elliptic curve and its associated torus.

Life   A game invented by John Conway, who called it the Game of Life, in which each cell on a square grid is designated as either alive or dead. In successive time steps or generations, each live cell survives or dies, and each dead cell remains dead or springs to life based on the status of their eight neighboring cells.

magic square An assignment of numbers to the cells of a 3×3 grid that are arranged into three rows and three columns so that each row, each column, and each diagonal produces the same sum.

manifold A surface satisfying general mathematical conditions.

mass action game A game that is repeatedly played by participants who do not necessarily act rationally and who may not know the full structure of the game but who accumulate information on the relative advantages of the available strategies.

Mathematica Mathematical computer software package created by Wolfram Research.

mathematical logic The branch of mathematics dealing with the laws of formal argumentation and consistent reasoning about abstract structures.

mathematical physics The branch of physics concerned with the development of mathematical theories to explain physical phenomena.

mechanics The branch of physics dealing with the laws of motion.

minimal spanning tree For a graph with n vertices, a set of $n - 1$ edges connecting all the vertices while having the smallest total length.

minimal surface A surface with minimum area that satisfies a specified set of conditions.

minimum Steiner tree A graph that improves on a minimal spanning tree by introducing new vertices and edges that result in a smaller total edge length.

modular form A type of elliptic curve that has well-behaved properties related to the curve's lattice.

Nash bargaining game A simple two-person game in which each player demands a portion of an available resource.

Nash equilibrium In game theory, a collection of strategies, one for each player, having the property that if all players follow these strategies, no individual player can improve his or her outcome by switching to a different strategy. Also known as a strategic equilibrium.

Nash program   A call by John Nash to reformulate cooperative games into the larger framework of noncooperative games.

natural number   One of the positive integers 1, 2, 3, 4, 5, ...

noncooperative game   A game in which each player selects one of finitely many strategies without consulting the other player(s) in order to obtain an outcome that is personally advantageous.

number theory   The mathematical study of the properties of positive integers.

octonions   A set of numbers that form an eight-dimensional generalization of the complex numbers.

open problem   A mathematical question that has not been solved.

optics   The branch of the physical sciences dealing with properties of light and vision.

orthogonal   Independent objects that have no redundancy as measured by an inner product operator.

partial differential equation   An equation involving the derivatives of a function of several variables.

path integrals   Methods for calculating the distance traveled by quantum particles.

periodic function   A function whose values repeat on a regular basis. A function $f(x)$ is a periodic function if there is some constant k, called its period, so that $f(x + k) = f(x)$ for all values of x.

Plateau's problem   A question named after physicist Joseph Plateau asking for the construction of a surface with minimum area that fits a given boundary.

polygon   A planar region bounded by segments. The segments bounding the polygon are its sides, and their endpoints are its vertices.

polyhedron   A solid bounded by polygons. The polygons bounding the polyhedron are its faces; the sides of the polygons are its edges; the vertices of the polygons are its vertices.

polynomial   An algebraic expression that is the sum of the products of numbers and variables.

positive mass conjecture   Proposal from Riemannian geometry and Einstein's general theory of relativity asserting that the sum of all the energy in the universe is positive.

positive number   Any number whose value is greater than zero.

postulate   See AXIOM.

power   See EXPONENT.

power series   A representation of a function as an infinite sum of terms in which each term includes a power of the variable.

prime number   An integer greater than 1 that cannot be divided by any positive integer other than itself and 1. The first few prime numbers are 2, 3, 5, 7, 11, 13, 17, ...

private key cryptography   A collection of techniques for sending messages in which the sender does not make public the process used to encrypt or decrypt a message.

probability theory   The branch of mathematics concerned with the systematic determination of numerical values to indicate the likelihood of the occurrence of events.

proof   The logical reasoning that establishes the validity of a theorem from definitions, axioms, and previously proved results.

proper divisor   For any positive integer, those smaller positive numbers that divide it.

public key cryptography   A collection of techniques developed in the late 20th century that allow the sender to make public the process used to encrypt a message without revealing how to decrypt it.

quantum theory   Branch of physics that explains the properties of atoms, molecules, light, and the radiation of small particles.

quaternions   A set of numbers that form a four-dimensional generalization of the complex numbers.

radiation shields   Protective layers that block gamma rays and other high-energy particles that are produced by nuclear reactions.

Ramsey theory   Area of combinatorics concerned with how large a collection of objects must be in order to guarantee that it satisfies particular conditions.

random   Numerical values are random if no one value can be predicted from the knowledge of the other values.

random graph   A graph in which the existence of an edge between any two vertices is randomly determined by a probability distribution.

rational game   A game that is played only once and in which the participants reason logically from knowledge of the full structure of the game.

rational number   A number that can be expressed as a ratio of two integers. Also known as a fraction.

real number   One of the set of numbers that includes zero, the positive and negative integers, the rationals, and the irrationals.

reciprocity law   For a pair of integers p and q, a reciprocity law indicates when an expression of the form x^n can be written as both $x^n = p + q \cdot j$ and $x^n = q + p \cdot k$ for some integers j and k.

recursive function   A function in which the value at each positive integer is defined in terms of its values at smaller positive integers.

root   (1) A solution to an equation. (2) A number that when repeatedly multiplied produces a given numerical value.

RSA algorithm   The standard for commercial public key cryptosystems that was created in 1977 by MIT scientists Ronald Rivest, Adi Shamir, and Leonard Adleman.

secure   An encryption algorithm is secure if messages encoded using the algorithm cannot be decoded without knowing the decryption matrix.

semistable elliptic curve   An elliptic curve whose three roots satisfy a particular condition involving prime numbers.

sequence   An infinitely long list of values that follow a pattern.

series   An infinite sum of numbers or terms.

set   A well-defined collection of objects.

set theory   The branch of mathematics dealing with relationships between sets.

signal processing   The branch of applied mathematics concerned with transmitting, manipulating, storing, and reconstructing electrical and electronic signals.

sine   For an acute angle in a right triangle, the ratio of the opposite side to the hypotenuse.

singularity   (1) Point at the center of a black hole where the curvature of space-time is infinite. (2) An irregularity where a surface has an undesirable property, usually related to the derivatives of the underlying function. Also known as a singular point.

singular point   See SINGULARITY.

smart cards   Plastic cards similar to credit cards that contain microprocessor chips enabling the cards to store information and modify that information during transactions.

special theory of relativity   A theory in physics developed by Albert Einstein to explain the properties of space, matter, and time.

spectral graph theory   Branch of graph theory concerned with the development and application of numerical measures that characterize the properties of graphs.

sphere   The set of all points in three-dimensional space at a given distance, called the radius, from a fixed point, called the center.

sphere packing   The mathematical analysis of the most efficient arrangement of equal-sized spheres into a space having a fixed volume.

Sprouts   A two-person game invented by John Conway played with pencil and paper. Starting with two dots on a piece of paper, players take turns joining any two dots with a curve that does not cross any curve already drawn and then add a new dot somewhere on the new curve.

square   (1) A four-sided polygon with all sides congruent to one another and all angles congruent to one another. (2) To multiply a quantity times itself; raise to the second power.

statistics   The branch of mathematics dealing with the collecting, tabulating, and summarizing numerical information obtained from observational or experimental studies and drawing conclusions about the population from which the data was selected.

strategic equilibrium   See NASH EQUILIBRIUM.

string theory   The theory from physics asserting that strings of matter form the fundamental building blocks of all substances.

surreal numbers   Numbers related to strategies in games that form a natural completion of the number system containing the integers, rationals, reals, complex, and transfinite numbers.

Sylver Coinage   A numbers game invented by John Conway in which two players take turns naming a positive integer as the value of a new coin that represents a monetary amount that cannot be generated by any combination of previously introduced coins.

tangent   (1) For an acute angle in a right triangle, the ratio of the opposite side to the adjacent side. (2) A line that touches a curve or surface indicating the direction of its curvature at the point of tangency.

tangle   One of the fundamental two-dimensional components of a mathematical knot.

theorem   A mathematical property or rule that has been proved.

thermodynamics   The branch of physics concerned with the study of heat and motion.

topology   The branch of mathematics concerned with the properties of geometrical surfaces.

transfinite number   A number that gives the cardinality of an infinite set.

triangle   A polygon with three vertices and three edges.

trigonometric functions   The functions $\sin(x)$, $\cos(x)$, and $\tan(x)$ that form the basis of the study of trigonometry.

trigonometry   The study of right triangles and the relationships among the measurements of their angles and sides.

uncountable   An infinite set is uncountable if it cannot be put into a one-to-one correspondence with the set of natural numbers.

variable   A letter used to represent an unknown or unspecified quantity.

variable threats game   A game in which a player can select one of a choice of penalties when the opponent deviates from the agreed-upon strategy.

vertex   The endpoint of a segment in a geometric figure.

wavelets   Irregular but basic wave forms that can be used to represent efficiently signals and images.

zero-sum game   A game in which competing participants make choices that result in payoffs for some players and penalties of equal magnitudes for the others.

FURTHER READING

Books

Ashurst, F. Gareth. *Founders of Modern Mathematics.* London: Muller, 1982. Biographies of selected prominent mathematicians.

Ball, W. W. Rouse. *A Short Account of the History of Mathematics.* New York: Dover, 1960. Reprint of 1908 edition of the classic history of mathematics covering the period from 600 B.C.E. to 1900.

Bell, Eric T. *Men of Mathematics.* New York: Simon and Schuster, 1965. The classic history of European mathematics from 1600 to 1900 organized around the lives of 30 influential mathematicians.

Boyer, Carl, and Uta Merzbach. *A History of Mathematics.* 2d ed. New York: Wiley, 1991. A history of mathematics organized by eras from prehistoric times through the mid-20th century; for more advanced audiences.

Burton, David M. *The History of Mathematics: An Introduction.* 2d ed. Dubuque, Iowa: Brown, 1988. Very readable college textbook on the history of mathematics through the end of the 19th century with biographical sketches throughout.

Dunham, William. *Journey through Genius: The Great Theorems of Mathematics.* New York: Wiley, 1990. Presentation of 12 mathematical ideas focusing on their historical development, the lives of the mathematicians involved, and the proofs of these theorems.

————. *The Mathematical Universe: An Alphabetical Journey through the Great Proofs, Problems, and Personalities.* New York: Wiley, 1994. Presentation of 26 topics in mathematics focusing on their historical development, the lives of the mathematicians involved, and the reasons these theorems are valid.

Eves, Howard. *Great Moments in Mathematics (After 1650).* Washington, D.C.: Mathematical Association of America, 1981. Presentation of major mathematical discoveries that occurred after 1650 and the mathematicians involved.

————. *Great Moments in Mathematics (Before 1650).* Washington, D.C.: Mathematical Association of America, 1983. Presentation of 20 major mathematical discoveries that occurred before 1650 and the mathematicians involved.

————. *An Introduction to the History of Mathematics.* 3d ed. New York: Holt, Rinehart and Winston, 1969. An undergraduate textbook covering the history of mathematical topics through elementary calculus, accessible to high school students.

Gillispie, Charles C., ed. *Dictionary of Scientific Biography.* 18 vols. New York: Scribner, 1970–80. Multivolume encyclopedia presenting biographies of thousands of mathematicians and scientists; for adult audiences.

Grinstein, Louise S., and Paul J. Campbell, eds. *Women of Mathematics: A Biobibliographic Sourcebook.* New York: Greenwood Press, 1987. Biographical profiles of 43 women, each with an extensive list of references.

Henderson, Harry. *Modern Mathematicians.* New York: Facts On File, 1996. Profiles of 13 mathematicians from the 19th and 20th centuries.

James, Ioan M. *Remarkable Mathematicians: From Euler to von Neumann.* Cambridge: Cambridge University Press, 2002. Profiles of 60 mathematicians from the 18th, 19th, and 20th centuries.

Katz, Victor J. *A History of Mathematics: An Introduction.* 2d ed. Reading, Mass.: Addison-Wesley Longman, 1998. College textbook that explains accessible portions of mathematical works and provides brief biographical sketches.

Morrow, Charlene, and Teri Perl, eds. *Notable Women in Mathematics: A Biographical Dictionary.* Westport, Conn.: Greenwood Press, 1998. Short biographies of 59 women mathematicians, including many 20th-century figures.

Muir, Jane. *Of Men and Numbers: The Story of the Great Mathematicians.* New York: Dover, 1996. Short profiles of mathematicians.

Newman, James R., ed. *The World of Mathematics.* 4 vols. New York: Simon and Schuster, 1956. Collection of essays about topics in mathematics, including the history of mathematics.

Osen, Lynn M. *Women in Mathematics.* Cambridge, Mass.: MIT Press, 1974. Biographies of eight women mathematicians through the early 20th century.

Perl, Teri. *Math Equals: Biographies of Women Mathematicians + Related Activities.* Menlo Park, Calif.: Addison-Wesley, 1978. Biographies of 10 women mathematicians through the early 20th century, each accompanied by exercises related to their mathematical work.

Reimer, Luetta, and Wilbert Reimer. *Mathematicians Are People, Too: Stories from the Lives of Great Mathematicians.* Parsippany, N.J.: Seymour, 1990. Collection of stories about 15 mathematicians with historical facts and fictionalized dialogue, intended for elementary school students.

———. *Mathematicians Are People, Too: Stories from the Lives of Great Mathematicians.* Vol. 2. Parsippany, N.J.: Seymour, 1995. Collection of stories about 15 more mathematicians with historical facts and fictionalized dialogue; intended for elementary school students.

———. *Historical Connections in Mathematics.* 2 vols. Fresno, Calif.: AIMS Educational Foundation, 1992–93. Each volume includes brief portraits of 10 mathematicians, with worksheets related to their mathematical discoveries, for elementary school students.

Stillwell, John. *Mathematics and Its History.* New York: Springer-Verlag, 1989. Undergraduate textbook organized around 20 topics, each developed in their historical context.

Struik, Dirk J. *A Concise History of Mathematics.* 4th rev. ed. New York: Dover, 1987. Brief history of mathematics through the first half of the 20th century, with extensive multilingual bio-graphical references.

———. *A Source Book in Mathematics, 1200–1800.* Cambridge, Mass.: Harvard University Press, 1969. Excerpts with commentary from 75 of the influential mathematical manuscripts of the period.

Tabak, John. *The History of Mathematics.* 5 vols. New York: Facts On File, 2004. Important events and prominent individuals in the development of the major branches of mathematics; for grades six and up.

Tanton, James. *Encyclopedia of Mathematics.* New York: Facts On File, 2005. Articles and essays about events, ideas, and people in mathematics; for grades nine and up.

Turnbull, Herbert W. *The Great Mathematicians.* New York: New York University Press, 1961. Profiles of six mathematicians with more detail than most sources.

Young, Robyn V., ed. *Notable Mathematicians: From Ancient Times to the Present.* Detroit, Mich.: Gale, 1998. Short profiles of mathematicians.

Internet Resources

Agnes Scott College. "Biographies of Women Mathematicians." Available online. URL: http://www.agnesscott.edu/lriddle/women/women.htm. Accessed March 4, 2005. Biographies of more than 100 women mathematicians prepared by students at Agnes Scott College, Decatur, Georgia.

Bellevue Community College. "Mathographies." Available online. URL: http://scidiv.bcc.ctc.edu/Math/MathFolks.html. Accessed March 4, 2005. Brief biographies of 25 mathematicians prepared by faculty members at Bellevue Community College, in Bellevue, Washington.

Drexel University. "Math Forum." Available online. URL: http://www.mathforum.org. Accessed March 3, 2005. Site for mathematics and mathematics education that includes "Problem of the Week," "Ask Dr. Math," and Historia-Matematica discussion group, by School of Education at Drexel University, in Philadelphia.

Miller, Jeff. "Images of Mathematicians on Postage Stamps." Available online. URL: http://jeff560.tripod.com. Accessed March 6, 2005. Images of hundreds of mathematicians and mathematical topics on international stamps, with links to mathematical stamp collectors, by high school math teacher Jeff Miller.

National Association of Mathematics. "Mathematicians of the African Diaspora." Available online. URL: http://www.math. buffalo.edu/mad. Accessed March 1, 2005. Includes profiles of 250 black mathematicians and historical information about mathematics in ancient Africa.

Rice University. "Galileo Project Catalog of the Scientific Community in the 16th and 17th Centuries." Available online. URL: http://galileo.rice.edu/lib/catalog.html. Accessed July 5, 2005. Biographical outlines of 600 member mathematicians and scientists of the period, compiled by the late professor Richard Westfall of Indiana University.

Scienceworld. "Eric Weisstein's World of Scientific Biography." Available online. URL: http://scienceworld.wolfram.com/ biography. Accessed February 12, 2005. Brief profiles of more than 250 mathematicians and hundreds of other scientists. Link to related site Mathworld, an interactive mathematics encyclopedia providing access to numerous articles about historical topics and extensive discussions of mathematical terms and ideas, by Eric Weisstein of Wolfram Research.

Simon Fraser University. "History of Mathematics." Available online. URL: http//www.math.sfu.ca/histmath. Accessed January 19, 2005. A collection of short profiles of a dozen mathematicians, from Simon Fraser University, Burnaby, British Columbia, Canada.

University of Saint Andrews. "MacTutor History of Mathematics Archive." Available online. URL: http://www-groups.dcs.st-andrews.ac.uk/~history. Accessed March 5, 2005. Searchable, online index of mathematical history and biographies of more than 2,000 mathematicians, from the University of Saint Andrews, Scotland.

University of Tennessee. "Math Archives." Available online. URL: http://archives.math.utk.edu/topics/history.html. Accessed

December 10, 2004. Ideas for teaching mathematics and links to Web sites about the history of mathematics and other mathematical topics, by the University of Tennessee, Knoxville.

Wikipedia: The Free Encyclopedia. "Mathematics." Available online. URL: http://en.wikipedia.org/wiki/Mathematics. Accessed August 22, 2005. Online biographies with many links to in-depth explanations of related mathematical topics.

ASSOCIATIONS

Association for Women in Mathematics, 4114 Computer and Space Sciences Building, University of Maryland, College Park, MD 20742-2461. Web site: http://www.awm-math.org. Telephone: (301) 405-7892. Professional society for female mathematics professors; Web site includes link to biographies of women in mathematics.

Mathematical Association of America, 1529 18th Street NW, Washington, DC 20036. Web site: http://www.maa.org. Telephone: (202) 387-5200. Professional society for college mathematics professors; Web site includes link to the association's History of Mathematics Special Interest Group (HOM SIGMAA).

National Association of Mathematicians, Department of Mathematics, 244 Mathematics Building, University at Buffalo, Buffalo, NY 14260-2900. Web site: http://www.math.buffalo.edu/mad/NAM. Professional society focusing on needs of underrepresented American minorities in mathematics.

National Council of Teachers of Mathematics, 1906 Association Drive, Reston, VA 20191-1502. Web site: http://www.nctm.org. Telephone: (703) 620-9840. Professional society for mathematics teachers.

Index